Healing

EMPTY HANDS

CANNON + ROSE PUBLISHING

COPYRIGHT © 2023 MORGAN MARTIN
Published by Cannon + Rose Publishing

ISBN   979-8-9866565-2-6   ebook
          979-8-9866565-0-2   paperback
          979-8-9866565-1-9   hardcover

Library of Congress Control Number: 2022913620

First Edition
Book Production and Publishing by Brands Through Books
brandsthroughbooks.com

Cover Photography: @alwaysautumnphotography
www.alwaysautumnphotography.com

Cannon + Rose logo artwork by Regina Potasnik
@scenes_from_the_soul

Unless otherwise indicated, all opening chapter Scripture references are taken from the New International Version (NIV) Bible.

www.healingemptyhands.com

EMPTY HANDS

FINDING HOPE AND PEACE
THROUGH MISCARRIAGE

MORGAN MARTIN

CANNON + ROSE
PUBLISHING

To the baby I'll never get to meet on this side of heaven: I promise to hold you in my heart until, one day, I can hold you in my hands.

And to my son, Brooks, who has shown me God's love, redemption, and grace in a fresh, new way.

CONTENTS

"I am with you and will watch over you wherever you go, and I will bring you back to this land. I will not leave you until I have done what I have promised you." —Genesis 28:15

BEFORE WE BEGIN . . .

WHEN YOUR HEART IS BROKEN, WHEN TRAGEDY STRIKES, who's the first person you turn to? I spent so many years of my life running to things and people that ultimately couldn't help me. In my past struggles, I turned to friends and family or stayed busy to stuff down my emotions. I thought that if I didn't take time to notice the feelings, they'd somehow just go away. But when I was told I was losing my baby, I immediately (and maybe for the first time) ran to Jesus first—not because I'm a Christian superstar, but because no one around me understood my pain. I had nowhere else to turn but to Jesus, so I did.

I was the first woman in my family, and the first one in my friend group, to have a miscarriage. On the one hand, I was thankful they'd never had to experience the pain I was going through. But at the same time, it left me feeling all alone. I felt isolated. And to make it worse, this tragedy was completely out of my control. Losing my baby wasn't a result of anything I'd done. It just *happened*, and it happened to me. And it would be safe to assume, since you're reading this, that it's happened to you too. My goal is that you don't have to feel isolated the way I did, lost and alone with no one to talk to about this.

Maybe no one around you understands the pain and suffering you're going through. Maybe they don't understand the weight of the loss, and that makes you feel dismissed or misunderstood. Maybe your family is on the other side of the spectrum—it's not that they *can't* understand, it's that they don't want to. Maybe they pretend like it never happened or that the pregnancy and your baby didn't matter, whether intentionally or unintentionally. And on their behalf, I'm so sorry. Your baby does matter, and your feelings are valid. If you're suffering this heartbreak alone—or maybe it just feels that way—I hope this book helps you feel a little less lonely. I understand exactly what you're going through, and I hope that you find comfort in that. You didn't ask for this to happen to you, and neither did I. But here we are, broken but together in this. And as I walk you through my journey, I hope I can help you find the same healing I've found in the arms of Jesus—the kind of healing that binds the deep crevices of my heart that I didn't even know were in need of mending.

Not only does no one understand my situation like God, no one understands *me* like God. He was the only one who could help me. He knit me together and created me in my mother's womb (Ps. 139:13 New International Version), and He cares so deeply for me and about the things that hurt me. Although you're probably reading this book in hopes of feeling understood (and I hope you do) or gaining clarity and wisdom on how to handle this grief (and I hope you do), I don't want this book to be the only place you run to. My ultimate goal is to point you to Christ, the only one who can heal our hurt and make sense of our mess.

According to research from March of Dimes, about 10 to 15 percent of pregnancies end in miscarriage. In fact, they say, "As many as half of all pregnancies may end in miscarriage. We don't know the exact number because a miscarriage may happen before a woman knows she's pregnant. Most women who miscarry go on to have a healthy pregnancy later" (March of Dimes 2017).

My goal in sharing this with you isn't to make you feel like a statistic. It's not to tell you that your pain should hurt less because miscarriages are so common. No, my goal is just to remind you that you're not alone in this experience, although it may feel that way. I wish I'd had a resource to help me feel understood and less alone when I was in the throes of my miscarriage and grief, but I didn't. That's why I wrote this book.

I won't have all the answers for you. I won't have any magic words or all the right things to say to make the pain go away. I wish I did. I can't personally heal you, though I hope to lead you toward healing through these pages. But there's a God who can. He can redeem our stories and our lives when we surrender our desires to Him. I'll show you some of the things He taught me in the midst of my deepest sorrow. I'll share with you the words I wish someone would've shared with me. As I do so, I pray the isolation you may be feeling melts away.

I promise to share my story and be vulnerable about the real things I went through. I promise to give you steps to deal with new pain, like seeing other women receive the blessing of a baby, and new healing, like how to navigate pregnancy after loss. I promise to be honest about the struggles I faced in hopes that you can know you're not alone. I understand you. I see you. I know the pain seems insurmountable. I know there are days when you feel like you could crumble at any given moment. I've been there too. But the pain you're going through, as messy as it is, has a purpose. God doesn't waste the pain we go through.

I don't know a lot because this world is filled with so much that's unknown. But what I am certain of, amid mountains of uncertainty, is this: God's promises for your life will come to pass.

"Not one of all the Lord's good promises to Israel failed; every one was fulfilled" (Joshua 21:45 NIV). My hope is to take you along the messy road I walked to learn how to have faith and strength when we don't see the promises of God fulfilled yet. Today is step one, and I'm glad you're here. Take this step toward healing together with me. Here we go.

CHAPTER ONE

SHATTERED HEARTS AND

EMPTY HANDS

"Be strong and courageous. Do not be afraid or terrified
. . . for the Lord your God goes with you; He will never
leave you nor forsake you."—Deuteronomy 31:6

A s MY HUSBAND AND I WALKED BACK TO OUR CAR, THE GLASS
doors of the hospital closed softly behind us. My vision became blurry, and a tear ran down my cheek. We had been so excited to bring home pictures of a little blob we were already so in love with, but instead, we heard the words "I'm so sorry" and left with tear-filled eyes, shattered hearts, and empty hands.

This began my journey down the hardest road I've ever walked . . .

* * *

Derek and I met in January of 2015 while working at a shoe store together in Michigan. I had moved to Michigan from my home state of Mississippi the year before, and Derek had worked at the store previously and then quit for an internship during his last year in college. But then he moved back to the area to finish one more class and met up with a friend for drinks, and that friend happened to be the guy who had originally interviewed me for the position.

When Derek mentioned he was looking for a part-time job, his friend encouraged him to work at the shoe store again because he thought we'd be a good match and wanted to set us up. I still remember meeting him in the back room of the shoe store when another coworker introduced us. Unbeknownst to me at the time, Derek left the store that afternoon and went to the gym with a bunch of his buddies, and that's when he told all of them that he was going to marry me. I wasn't interested in him at first, but he was persistent—and it turned out he was right. To this day, Derek is the most amazing man I've ever had the privilege of knowing.

We were instantly friends, and we started dating later that summer. We were together for three years before getting engaged in February of 2018, and he proposed on the pier at Lake Michigan, overlooking the frozen waves. It was magical. We got married exactly six months later, on August 24, 2018. In front of God, our family, and friends, we recited the words "for better or worse, in sickness and in health." Of course, we had no idea the weight those words would carry just two years later.

We knew we wanted kids from the very beginning. On our first date at Buffalo Wild Wings (I know, *I know*, but we were total bros working at a sneaker store before we dated), we talked about how we both wanted three children of our own and to adopt one. I was blown away by how similar we were! Later in our relationship, we would always talk about what we thought our kids might look like or who we hoped they'd become.

We joked about how we hoped they'd have my taste buds because Derek is just as picky of an eater as the two-year-old I used to babysit. I always hoped they'd have his witty sense of humor; his thick, dark hair; and his bright-blue eyes. He wanted our babies to have my drive (my motivation . . . not the way I drive, let's be clear) and my little button nose. I wanted them to have his patience and wisdom. We had it all thought out down to every detail and dreamed of what our future family would be like one day.

In August of 2020, on a ten-day trip out west to celebrate our two-year wedding anniversary, we decided that we were ready to start our family. The very next month, we found out we were expecting. The news was more exciting than I had ever anticipated, and I couldn't wait to surprise Derek with it. When he came home from work that night, I had a tiny, gray newborn onesie with little sheep on it and a letterboard that read, "Baby Martin Coming June 2021." My longing to become a mom was finally being realized, and my husband was going to be the best dad. We told my husband's family right away because we just couldn't contain our excitement. My parents' birthdays are both in early October, so we booked a last-minute trip and flew down south to Tennessee and Mississippi (where I grew up) to see them. We told each of them the news in fun, special ways. We told our closest friends individually. Everyone was bursting with excitement for us.

We never expected that, just ten days later, we would receive the most devastating news of our lives.

BLACK BOOTS AND DUSTY FLOORBOARDS

It was the morning of October 28, 2020. My eyes peered open before the sun could peak through our bedroom window. Butterflies filled my stomach as I lay awake in the dark, waiting for my alarm to go off. My husband lay fast asleep next to me. I stared at the black space above me and imagined what the ultrasound would look like, what the *thud-thud-thud* of the heartbeat would sound like. The butterflies fluttered. I wondered if I would cry happy tears or just be so overjoyed that I would forget to have any expression at all. A quick, high-pitched tone rang from my phone. Before the first chime could even finish, I flopped over the side of the bed—not very gracefully, I might add—and pressed the *Alarm Off* button. I sprang to my feet and got dressed. I remember wanting to dress up for the ultrasound. I wanted to look presentable when we Face-Timed my unsuspecting friends and family later that day with the exciting news of our growing family! I wore a thin, white sweater with navy-blue stripes, black skinny jeans, and black heeled booties.

By the time we left the house, the sun had come up, and my butterflies seemed to have multiplied. I remember riding in the passenger seat of my husband's truck. With the sun beaming on my face, I looked at my husband, and we silently grinned a nervous but excited grin at each other. When we arrived at the OB-GYN's office, my husband dropped me off at the door since it was so chilly that morning. I walked along the concrete path, past the frost-covered grass that glimmered in the sun. My anticipation grew with every single step I took toward those glass doors. Even through my COVID-protocol mask, I could smell that familiar doctor's office smell as I opened the door. I walked to the counter and spoke with the lady behind the glass to check in. I found a seat on a black and gray doctor's office chair. My husband walked in, joined me, and held my hand.

A young, blonde ultrasound technician with a small, perky bun on top of her head interrupted the weatherman on the TV above our heads when she opened the door and called out my name as if it were a question: "Morgan Martin?"

As I stood up, I smiled at her with my eyes, and my husband

and I followed her into a dark room in the corner of the building. "We will be right in here," she said, shutting the door behind us. The small, dim room was lit up only by a small screen connected to an ultrasound machine. I set my purse down and handed my phone to my husband. I said, "Take pictures or videos so we can show our parents later!"

I proceeded to lie down on the tan leather seat in the center of the room. My butterflies had turned into a nervous stomachache as I reclined back. My skin was chilled. The jelly on the ultrasound wand was warm on my belly. I glanced over at Derek with a glimmer of nervous excitement in my eyes. The monitor was turned to face the ultrasound tech. I heard a swooshing sound as she explained that she'd be looking at the health of the ovaries and uterus first. She continued to move the wand around and click buttons on the keyboard. It took her what seemed like forever to say anything. She just kept moving the wand around my belly and pressing into my abdomen just a bit harder. I could tell something was wrong. She wasn't speaking. When she finally did, she said, "Are you sure you know the date of your last missed period?"

I paused before I spoke. Then, confused, I uttered back, "Um, yes, I'm sure. We were trying for this baby, so we were careful about keeping track of everything." My first thought was, *Wow, I must be farther along than I thought.* I had heard of women going nine months without knowing they were pregnant, so me going an extra month or two without knowing wouldn't have been the world's most bizarre story . . . The technician didn't reply. *Click click, swoosh swoosh.* She finally turned the monitor toward me and, with a crack in her voice, said words like "anembryonic pregnancy" and "possible miscarriage" and "I'm so sorry."

Her words sounded like a muffled echo, as if someone had stuffed cotton balls into my ears and put me in a long, dark, empty tunnel. I tried to make out the rest of what she said, but all I could think about was how it had to be a mistake. Maybe it was her first day on the job. Maybe she was inexperienced. That would explain the misunderstanding. Because this clearly *had* to be a misunderstanding. I mean, this wasn't supposed to happen to me.

I just remember thinking, *This isn't happening. This can't be happening.*

She ended the conversation by saying, "Your OB will look over the ultrasound and call you with an official diagnosis and will likely want to see you again in a week for a closer look to see if anything changes between now and then."

My husband calmly replied to the blonde lady with the perky bun, and she slowly exited the room with her head down. I stood up on heavy legs that seemed to move on their own. I didn't have the brain capacity in that moment to consciously function. Everything was on autopilot. I used the coarse white tissue paper the chair was covered in to wipe off the jelly. I was so in shock that I didn't even cry. I just stared blankly ahead, my eyes wide and unblinking. I buttoned my pants and took two steps toward my husband. When our eyes met, I fell to my knees, and that's when I began to sob. I just kept saying, "This can't be happening. This can't be happening."

Everything after that was a blur: Putting my black-heeled booties back on. Walking out of the small hospital room. It was an out-of-body experience. It seemed like I was just standing still, watching someone else go about their day in slow motion. I came back into myself the moment those silver doors separated and let in the bone-chilling breeze of the cold October morning. We walked back to the truck, brokenhearted, confused, and silent. My husband opened my passenger-side door for me. I climbed inside and put my black boots on the dusty floorboard as he shut the door behind me.

ROLLER COASTERS AND CROWDED ROOMS

Starting on that cold morning in October, I began to learn an important lesson: pain is messy and usually comes without warning.

After we found out we lost the baby, I felt a flood of emotions all at once. Some were feelings I had never felt before. I was sad and confused. I was jarred and shocked, like I had hit a speed bump at 65 mph with no idea it was coming. The news was shocking and devastating. It was raw and unfiltered. I didn't invite those emotions in, but somehow, they showed up anyway with suitcases as if to say they'd be here a while.

The emotions I felt were a roller coaster. Sometimes I felt everything all at once, and other times I was so numb to the pain I felt nothing at all. What I've realized is that there's truly no right or wrong way to feel in these moments, friend. The best gift we can give ourselves in times like these is truly just *grace*. If you're anything like me, you're hard on yourself, and it's hard for you to extend grace to yourself.

Just a few weeks after hearing the news, I remember thinking, *Wow, Morgan. It's been five weeks already, and you're still crying about this. That's embarrassing. You should be healed by now and more "normal" than this.* I had no sympathy for myself and the newness of all the emotions I was feeling. I wish I had been kinder to myself. Looking back, I wish I would've given myself grace as I navigated those treacherous waters for the first time. If I could do it all over again, I would be gentler with myself and remove any expectations I had surrounding my healing. Healing is an awkward process. It's not pretty, and it's not a straight line. It's messy.

As we try to pick up the pieces and continue forward, we move from the initial hurt into the in-between place. That middle area of moving on is awkward and unfamiliar. It's the space of "already but not yet." It's a gray area, a desert. I had an identity crisis for months following the news of my miscarriage because I didn't feel like I fit in anywhere. Everything just felt blurry.

It was as if I was in a crowded room full of people where everyone knew each other and was talking to each other, but no one knew me. No one wanted to know me. And certainly, no one was talking to me. That's the kind of isolation I felt. It's like they were all huddled together shoulder to shoulder with their backs turned toward me. And there I was, standing in the middle of the crowded room all alone, wondering where I fit in. But I didn't fit in. I couldn't. It was like life was moving on without me, and I was left standing in the center of that room for months. By myself.

No one knew who I was . . . including me.

CHAPTER TWO

THE HILLS AND THE VALLEYS

"You intended to harm me, but God intended it for good
to accomplish what is now being done, the saving of
many lives."—Genesis 50:20

T HERE WE WERE, IN THE PARKING LOT OUTSIDE THE OB-GYN'S
office, having just received the worst news of our lives. I
stared through the windshield of my husband's truck as he climbed
into the driver's side. I studied the grooves in the orange brick
along the building's wall until it all became blurry. I blinked, and
tears streamed from my eyes, down my cheeks and onto my sweater. I just kept saying that there had to be a mistake; this couldn't
be happening to us. My husband mentioned what the ultrasound
tech told us about the follow-up ultrasound and insinuated that
meant there was hope. We really didn't need to panic yet. After
what seemed like hours but was probably more like thirty minutes,
we finally agreed to go home, get comfy, and sort through our
emotions where we felt safe. Where it was familiar.

As we drove down the same roads we had just driven down
not even two hours before, everything somehow seemed completely different. Those same roads I'd traveled thousands of times suddenly felt heavy. The last time I had driven down that road, I'd
been so hopeful. I was on my way to see my baby on an ultrasound
for the first time. It was different now.

It was totally strange to me how our world had just stopped, yet for everyone else, it still spun the same. We passed other cars as we drove along, and all I could think about was how badly I wanted to be any of those people. In that moment, I wanted to be anyone but me. The people all around us were having a normal Wednesday. We stopped at the same traffic light we had stopped at just hours before. This time, the butterflies had dissipated, leaving behind a big, open pit in the bottom of my stomach. A woman in the car to the left of us was wearing sunglasses and singing to a song on the radio. The men sitting inside the work truck to our right were talking and laughing together. I had never felt more unseen, forgotten, or lonely as I did in that moment. How could I believe that God was still good? Would I ever be able to trust Him again? Could I find strength in the truth of His words despite this devastating loss? It was the first and only time in my life I ever truly questioned if God had forgotten about me. As we pulled into the driveway, got out, and walked through the garage door of our home, I saw everything differently. Just hours ago, I had walked through that same door as a hope-filled woman anticipating one of the greatest days of her life. My husband had no choice but to leave for work shortly after we got back home, as he had only taken off that morning to be with me at the ultrasound. So, I was home alone. I sat on the couch and stared at our fireplace, which wasn't even lit. It was just a black box with a screen between me and the gas logs inside. I must've sat there in a daze for an hour before reaching for my phone. When I did, I opened up Instagram. I'm not sure if it was because I wanted to get my mind off my misery and onto something else, anything else that could distract me, or because it was just habit to grab my phone and get on social media. Either way, the first thing that loaded on my Instagram was a reel from a friend who I didn't even know had had a miscarriage, posting about her story. Oh, hey God. I see you.

On her reel, she shared that she had lost her baby on Thanksgiving Day the year before and gone into the doctor's office shortly after with stomach pains only to find out she was pregnant again with her "rainbow baby." She shared in the caption how she had just given birth to her son. She talked about how Thanksgiving next month would be better than last year's. It brought me to tears. In the background of the reel was a song I had heard once before but didn't honestly think much of until it was put into the context of something tragic and painful that I was now facing myself. The song was "Hills and Valleys" by Tauren Wells. As I listened to the song, the chorus cut me to my core because it was what I had been questioning all day long. The chorus of this song talks about how, when we are on the mountaintops of life, we should humbly give honor and glory to the one who allowed us to be in that position. And in the valleys of life, we should lift our eyes to remember the one who hasn't left our side, the one who still sees us there even at our lowest of lows. *Sees me there.* I *was* seen after all.

WAVES AND WHIRLWINDS

For the last few hours since my ultrasound, I had felt so unseen. I felt like God had allowed this to happen to me because He somehow forgot about me for a split second, that maybe He didn't catch this in time. Maybe He meant to intervene but got busy? I wondered if maybe God had asked Siri to put a reminder in His calendar to "check back later and stop the pain before it happened," but it was too late. Or maybe this problem was too small for Him, too minuscule to matter. I mean, there were more pressing things happening in the world. In the grand scheme of things, I was only one human, so maybe I just didn't make the high-priority list that day.

Of course, I knew in my heart that none of those things were true, but in the moment, those panicked, lonely thoughts swirled through my head at rapid speed like a whirlwind. I now know the character of God too well to truly believe that this happened without Him knowing or that He could have the capacity to forget. But I was so disoriented and shocked that I felt, in those moments, like I didn't matter enough for God to save me from my heartbreak.

Maybe you've been there too. Maybe you're there now. Not only do I see you and understand your pain, but God sees you too, in the midst of your heartbreak that seems insurmountable.

Through the lyrics of the song "Hills and Valleys," God's gentle voice whispered His truth to me in response to my thoughts. I was loved, and I wasn't forgotten. I was seen and valued. My pain didn't negate His attention to detail in my life. A feeling of peace washed over me, and I rested in it.

But almost as quickly as that peace overcame me, like a refreshing wave on a hot day at the beach, the next wave came out of nowhere. This time, it wasn't a refreshing one. It was a wave that smashed into me, the kind of wave that flips you around without warning. My next thought was, *Okay, wait. So, if God does see me, and this song is a reminder of that, then why on earth did He allow this to happen?* That question haunted me for hours. I just sat on my couch, listened to the lyrics of that song on repeat, and journaled all of my thoughts and emotions to our Lord. Most of my journal consisted of questions like "why *me*," "why did this happen to *me*," and "why did you choose *me*?"

I've often wondered what God must've thought in those moments of my grief and questioning. I wondered if He was angry that I would question Him or his authority. I wondered if He was hurt, as the good Father He is, that I would question His love for me. The Bible tells us that God delights in us (Ps. 147:11 NIV). When His children confide in Him and bring Him our deepest, darkest parts of ourselves, He meets us right where we are. He's there in the pain, the chaos, the confusion. The questions we ask in our heads but don't dare say out loud, He already knows them. He created our inmost being (Ps. 139:13 NIV) and knows us better than anyone else. Trying to put up a façade or brushing off the pain doesn't work with God, and neither does trying to jump too quickly to the "everything is fine" part of the healing process.

Pain is messy, and if anyone knows that, it's Jesus. He was fully God yet fully man. He was fully holy and also fully human. Because of that, the Bible says, "We do not have a high priest who is unable to empathize with our weaknesses" (Heb. 4:15 NIV). He understands. Jesus had His fair share of heartache and betrayal in His earthly life. I truly believe that He desires that we come to Him honestly with our feelings and emotions instead of trying to heal without Him, even if we feel like those emotions are too harsh or too raw. Sometimes, I feel like I need to clean up my emotions before I come to God with them because if I just said what I was thinking, it would be too "bad" to say out loud. The truth is that God can handle the sharp, piercing questions that roll off our tongues. So, when I was honest with God about my exact feelings and my emotions in those moments as I journaled, I sat and waited for answers. "Why, God?" I asked over and over. I didn't get a response.

ASSIGNMENTS AND INTENTIONS

I remember sitting in our backyard that evening with my husband and our golden retriever. Sitting by the fire pit in the cool Autumn air with the smell of wood burning is one of our favorite fall activities. Derek lit a fire for us after he got home from work in hopes that it would make us feel better. As I sat there, watching the sun go down and the stars peek out of a dark-blue sky, I asked again, *Why God?* This time, I felt his voice as He simply and clearly replied back to me, *Because I know you'll use it.* In that moment, my perspective shifted from seeing this as a tragedy happening *to* me to an assignment by God happening *for* me. Don't misunderstand me, though. That didn't mean God caused my miscarriage. But I do believe He allowed it to happen to me and that He had a plan to use it for good.

It reminded me of the story of Joseph in the Bible. Joseph was his father, Jacob's, favorite son. This made all of Joseph's brothers so angry that they didn't speak to him. Then Joseph started receiving dreams from the Lord, and when he told his brothers about the dreams, they despised him even more. One day, Joseph went to go find his brothers while they were tending their flocks, and as they saw him approaching, they plotted to harm him. They stripped Joseph of the colorful robe their father had gifted him and threw him into an empty pit. Then the brothers sold him to Midianites, who then sold Joseph to Potiphar, one of Pharaoh's officials and the captain of the guard.

Joseph eventually won over the affection of Potiphar. Unfortunately for him, Joseph also won over the affection of Potiphar's wife. When Joseph refused to be intimate with her, she lied and told her husband that Joseph tried to sexually assault her. Then Potiphar threw Joseph into prison. There, he interpreted the dream of a cupbearer, and years later, of the Pharaoh too. Afterward, "Pharaoh said to Joseph, 'Since God has made all this known to you, there is no one so discerning and wise as you. You shall be in charge of my palace, and all my people are to submit to your orders. Only with respect to the throne will I be greater than you.' So Pharaoh said to Joseph, 'I hereby put you in charge of the whole land of Egypt.'" (Gen. 41:39–41 NIV).

The land of Egypt was abundant under Joseph's rule, but there was famine everywhere else, including Canaan—where his family still lived. So, Joseph's brothers went to Egypt twice to buy grain from Joseph, but they didn't recognize him when they saw him. Joseph was extremely kind to his brothers and even feasted with them. In Genesis 45, he makes himself known to his brothers, and they weep. The story continues, and the whole family reunites. Joseph's brothers apologize to him and offer themselves as his slaves for what they had done to him. His life had been turned upside down for twenty years. He had been betrayed, falsely accused, imprisoned, and forgotten. Joseph could've made them pay. He could've questioned God. Of all the things Joseph could have done or said, he replied to his brothers, "You intended to harm me, but God intended it for good to accomplish what is now being done, the saving of many lives" (Gen. 50:20 NIV).

"God intended it for good" (Gen. 50:20 NIV). Purpose. That was the first time I caught a glimpse that there would be purpose in my pain. But of course, I didn't know what that would look like at the time. I began to see evidence that there would eventually be something good that came from this. I knew God allowed this to happen because I would use it—the pain, the hurt, the trauma.

Not only would I use it, but I wanted to use it. I needed this pain to not be for nothing. But can I be honest? In that moment, I would've settled for a little less purpose if that meant I could have my baby back. Just because I knew there would be good that came from my pain didn't make the pain hurt any less. It was devastating, and that's why I'm so captivated by Joseph and his response to his own serious struggles.

Joseph saw the good in his terrible situation. He had faith that God would restore everything to him that was lost. Joseph had every reason to feel hopeless, afraid, and forgotten, and I'm sure, at times, he did. But Joseph really believed God's faith never left him. And because of that, God used Joseph's pain to save the lives of many.

He can use our pain the same way too. Even though I know it doesn't feel like it right now, there's hope in the pain you're facing. God didn't cause tragedy to happen to you or to me or to Joseph, but He can still use it for good. Joseph's pain wasn't for nothing, my pain wasn't for nothing, and neither is yours. This is all for *something*—even if you can't see that yet.

Isn't it crazy that God uses everything for our good? I mean, really, *everything*? That's easy to say when the sun is shining, and life is going almost perfectly. It's in the earth-shattering moments of life and loss that it's harder to fathom. The kind of moments where your legs feel too heavy to get out of bed and face the day. That's how I felt on many days following the loss of my baby. But no matter what your situation is, God promises to work everything for our good.

After studying and meditating on Romans 8:28 (NIV), I noticed it says that God "works for the good." I used to read that as if the Lord was going to *turn* situations good. But that would imply that these things happened out of His control. Turning it for good would mean that things happen, and God says, "Oh wait, I totally forgot about Morgan today, and something awful has happened. Now what are we going to do?" But it's not like that at all, is it? He's a sovereign God who's in full control, knowing everything that will happen to us before it does and not causing it but allowing it, knowing full well that in doing so, He can and *will* use that pain for good. He doesn't have to *turn* it good; it already is. He already has a plan for it to be good, even when we don't see it, because God doesn't waste pain.

I hope the Lord will reveal to you some ways in which you can use the heartache you're feeling to help others, that you'll find ways to use your pain and not waste it. What does "good" look like for you? What are some ways you can think of to actively start using this pain for good? Or what are some of the ways you already have? If you could pick your own version of this messy pain turning out "good," what would you choose? What would that look like?

CHAPTER THREE

FOLLOW-UPS AND

FALSE STARTS

"That is why, for Christ's sake, I delight in weaknesses,
in insults, in hardships, in persecutions, in
difficulties. For when I am weak, then I am strong."
—2 Corinthians 12:10

LATER THAT NIGHT, A FEW HOURS AFTER OUR ULTRASOUND, MY husband and I called our parents to tell them the devastating news. We wanted to wait until they were home from work to let them know what had happened. We called my mom first, then my dad, and then Derek's parents. My mom had already been praying. She knew something was wrong when she didn't hear from us right after the ultrasound. The hardest part was having to untell them about the grandchild they were going to have but now wouldn't. It was so painful for us to relive those moments again just hours later. The feelings I felt in the ultrasound room came flooding back to me all at once. It was like ripping open a wound that hadn't even begun to heal yet. I couldn't wrap my mind around not having the baby we had been dreaming about for weeks and praying about for even longer than that. I sobbed again. I just couldn't accept what the doctors told me. A part of me felt that if I just didn't believe it was true, then maybe it wouldn't be. Our parents were in just as much pain as we were, both for the loss of the baby and for the pain they saw us having to go through.

Early the next day, my OB called us and diagnosed us with a possible anembryonic pregnancy. This happens when an embryo doesn't develop or stops developing, and the reason is often unknown. After "confirming" what the ultrasound technician saw was accurate, the doctor said that she wanted to do another ultrasound the following week. In these types of cases, one ultrasound can be inconclusive. So, to be safe and make sure they weren't missing anything, they wanted to schedule a follow-up. Knowing that there was another ultrasound appointment coming up gave me a reason to hope that there was a mistake and to pray for a miracle.

Our parents checked in on us often during the days after our first ultrasound. My mother-in-law told me that she had done some research on anembryonic pregnancies and found several online forums where the mothers had been diagnosed with it, just like me. These forums were filled with hundreds of stories of women whose babies had just been in a weird position during the initial ultrasound. In later ultrasounds, they found a heartbeat and a healthy baby. My mother-in-law presented us with this information "with fear and trembling," she said, because she didn't want to get our hopes up only to be crushed all over again.

We knew our parents didn't want to accept this horrible news either, so they were researching possible misunderstandings and praying alongside us. How I longed to be one of the women on those forums someday. I'd share all about this silly misunderstanding and send in a picture of my cute little baby sitting up in one of the outfits I had already bought before our ultrasound.

The week that followed was excruciating. We had no answers. I was praying for a miracle, and I thought that I would get one. I thought the reason I'd "use this pain" was to show how God could perform a miracle and give me a baby everyone thought I wouldn't get to have. The doctors hadn't seemed hopeful of a diagnosis change, but I was. I had faith that everything would be different—better—when I went for my follow-up ultrasound.

On Halloween, we had a fundraising event at our gym to support the Special Olympics. I had registered to be on a workout team for the event about a month before. We donated money, and Derek went to work out for the cause, but I decided not to physically participate in the event. Everyone asked about me that day, and my husband covered for me by saying I wasn't feeling well, which was true because I was just so worn down by my grief.

If I can be honest with you, the main reason I didn't show up that day was that I was embarrassed. People I had told about our pregnancy who knew about our miscarriage were going to be there. I couldn't face them. I just wanted to hide. I was so embarrassed that I had told them just days before that we were expecting and how ready we were to become parents. They had celebrated with us and were so excited to be honorary aunts and uncles. But then, just days later, we had to untell them too. I felt stupid for telling them so soon. I felt humiliated that my body had failed me. I felt like a failure of a woman because my body couldn't and didn't do what it was "supposed" to. I was so numb, and I couldn't bear the thought of having to face them again so soon. I isolated myself for that entire week. I just wanted to hide under the covers and wake up from the nightmare that had become my harsh reality.

The truth is my friends never made me feel the way I did in those moments. Our community rallied around us when we needed them most. They loved us so well during our loss. They rejoiced with us in our happiness when we shared the news of our pregnancy and equally bore the weight of our grief for our loss as if it were their own. They were there for us in every way. They went above and beyond to remind us they cared. They sat and cried with us. They brought us food. They sent gifts and flowers. They texted me often just to ask how I was doing. They showed up big for us in their own unique ways, and I'll never forget how loved I felt in the midst of the hardest moment of my life.

The hardest part of all of that was letting them show up for me. I constantly had to fight off the feeling that I was an inconvenience to them because of my grief. I had to battle the thought that I needed to rush through healing to get better so that I could have a better response to their "how are you today?" text than I did last week. I had to battle the feeling that I had to lie about how I was doing so that I didn't burden them with my feelings. I'm someone who doesn't like talking about feelings or emotions or asking for help. I had to learn how to do all three during this season. Looking back, I see that it was absolutely necessary for my healing. Pretending to be better than I was would've just been a lie, a total false start.

ACCEPTANCE AND ISOLATION

It took a lot of growing as a person to even accept anyone's help. I'm someone who would rather pretend everything's okay so I can move on to lighter things. I don't like sitting with my emotions or processing them most of the time. I'm like a machine in the sense that I can power through anything that comes my way and not let it rattle me too much. I don't like crying in front of anyone, and I sometimes view grief as something to accomplish, like if I move through it and feel "better" by a certain time frame, then I will "win" at grief. It may seem like I have it all together since I can just power through the worst situations as if nothing ever happened, but the reality is just the opposite. Pain isn't easy for me. The truth is that grief is actually really hard for me to work through. It's hard for me to intentionally take the effort or make the time to work through it, and that's why I try to pretend it doesn't exist.

I like to paint this picture of having it all together and being strong and capable, which makes it very hard to accept help because I see myself as weak when I do. But I learned the value of accepting help from others instead of pushing it away, mostly because my closest friends forced me to accept their help—with love, of course. I learned that it's not just okay but normal *not* to have it all together all the time. The people around you love you and don't want you to go through this alone, so don't be afraid to let your people in and be open to sharing what you're going through.

I feel like it's hard for women, in general, to ask for or accept help. But even if it's not natural for you, just like it isn't for me, I encourage you from the bottom of my heart not to feel bad about asking for help when you need it. Maybe that looks like asking for help on a project at work that the "old you" would have accomplished in a few hours but that you now need some help to complete by the deadline. Maybe you have children at home, and asking for help looks like calling a friend who's getting her own kids from school that afternoon and asking her to pick yours up too, so you don't have to.

Advocate for yourself and what you need, even if that's just space. Remember that part of saying what you need and asking for help looks like saying no to things. If it's something that requires more than you have to give right now, say no. You can just say no to the things that don't serve you or fill you up. Just because you could do those things doesn't mean you should. No one benefits when we try to pour from an empty cup. In certain seasons, it's important to say no so that we can fill ourselves up in order to pour out more to help others later on. And since you're starting out with a cup that's emptier than usual, it may take a little more time and attention than before to fill you up the way you're used to.

I once heard someone say that "no" is a full sentence and doesn't require an explanation. Set boundaries and realistic expectations for those around you! Maybe that's letting your child's school know that you can't head up the fundraiser next month, and someone else should take the lead until you're ready to jump back in. Maybe that's letting your husband know you'll be having leftovers or eating out a few days more than normal each week. Set those expectations and allow yourself to say no when you need to.

On the opposite side of that boundary, I think it's equally important to allow yourself to say yes to some things to avoid isolation. The worst thing you can be right now is isolated. The best asset you have is your community. I know that it may seem like I'm speaking out of both sides of my mouth or contradicting myself, but yes and no actually go hand in hand. They're not mutually exclusive. They both serve you on different days and at different times of each day. There's a balance to saying no and saying yes in your season of grief. Say yes to a day with your friends, or maybe even be the one to initiate it. Even if you're not feeling up to it on the morning of your plans, show up and let yourself laugh, have fun, and forget about the heartache you're going through for a few minutes. Just be you. And feel the freedom to say yes to things that help you cope. Surround yourself with the people who not only want to see you get through this but want to *help* you get through this as well. Take inventory each day and decide what it is you need in that moment—whether it's time to say no or time to say yes.

If you don't have a community of loving, supportive people around you right now, I encourage you to find one or create one. I found it helpful to plug into Facebook groups for moms who have had miscarriages, which provided an online community and support. Maybe you can find a hobby and a group that meets together to participate in that hobby. For example, my mother-in-law loves scrapbooking, and she's part of a group that gets together every few months to scrapbook for an entire weekend. Maybe find fun painting or culinary classes you can take to get started on a new activity or to get out of the house and do something that interests you. Find a place to volunteer. This will help you take the focus off yourself and help others at the same time, which will make you feel *so* good. Find a Bible study group at your church or maybe a book club. You could join a gym or take up yoga. These are just a few ideas to help you create a community if you don't have one right now.

GRIEF STYLES AND GREEN LIGHTS

It's very likely you're going through this experience with a spouse or partner. And maybe your question is, what if they don't grieve the same way I do? One of my biggest supporters and a key person in my community after my miscarriage was my husband. He was my rock, and I wanted to be his. After all, our spouse or partner experiences this pain with us as much as we do.

My husband and I cope very differently, and I know that's really common in relationships, so I think it's worth mentioning here. I'm an external processor. That just means that I process my thoughts by talking about them out loud, usually with someone else or sometimes by journaling. Derek is an internal processor, which means he'd rather die than tell me how he truly feels until he's sorted out and worked through all of his emotions. He would rather wait until he's okay to talk about what he's gone through and the emotions he was feeling.

Years before our miscarriage, Derek's uncle passed away very unexpectedly in the summer of 2016. It was the first time in our relationship that I had to watch Derek grieve. It honestly jarred me a little because I remember him not speaking almost at all for days. He just sat there in a daze, surrounded by friends and family, and wouldn't utter a word. He'd give a half-smile here or there or answer someone's question so as not to be rude, but otherwise, he kept to himself.

Others in his family coped by telling funny stories and fond memories. I related more to their grieving style, as it was more familiar and similar to my own. I didn't understand why Derek kept to himself so much. I wasn't expecting him to "get over" this pain or grief by pressing him to begin talking again. The goal wasn't to get back to normal as fast as possible or anything like that. It was just a confusing time for me because I wanted to be there for him. I wanted to comfort him but didn't know how to best serve him in those moments because his grieving style was so different from mine.

On the day of the funeral, he started to get back to his normal self again. He was back to being lighthearted and seemed like the person I knew. Finally, about a week after the funeral, Derek brought up how he had been feeling those days, and we talked about all that had happened. He was finally in a place where he was ready to talk about it. That's when he explained that, in times of crisis or grief, he needs space and time to process his emotions silently and alone.

Had we not gone through that experience where I learned to understand his thought process and the heart behind his silence before our miscarriage, I could have easily seen his silence during that time as indifference. If I hadn't seen him grieve in the past, I would've probably pushed him to open up and talk through his thoughts with me because, in my mind, that's what's most helpful. He would have resisted doing that because it wasn't in line with being true to himself and the things *he* needs when he's hurting. He's not an external processor like me. And I would've seen his resistance as him not caring and not wanting to get better. I also surely would've tried to talk out all my feelings with him and been frustrated when he didn't reciprocate by telling me all of his feelings right then too. This would've just been another false start on the road to healing and would have taken us down a path full of much more fighting and heartache.

But because we had gone through some level of trauma or hurt in the past and talked through what we each needed in that moment, we grew to understand each other better. That level of understanding helped us cope with each other's grieving styles in the midst of our miscarriage. I understood what he needed from me and what I could realistically expect from him. What that looked like, practically, was me giving him space to process through things on his own, not pressing issues he wasn't ready to talk about, and sharing my feelings without expecting him to pour his heart out in return when I finished.

He knew what I needed, so he tried his best to often ask me how I was doing and feeling to give me a green light and a space to share openly without fear that I would overwhelm him. Then, once we had both had time, we could openly talk about things with each other. Derek opened up and shared his thoughts and feelings with me once he had sorted through them because he felt ready and wasn't rushed to do so by me. This makes us sound perfect, but I pinky promise we aren't, and there were definitely bumps in the road, but building that foundation helped us a lot during our miscarriage.

It's so important to remember that, even though we're going through this physically as women, our husbands or partners are still going through this pain too. We just wear our pain differently. They weren't pregnant and didn't go through the same physical pain we did, but they're experiencing that same pain emotionally. They lost a child too. I know it was easy for me to get so lost in my feelings and my own pain and emotions that I sometimes forgot to check in on Derek and ask what he needed or how I could be there for him. My husband didn't personally need much, if any-thing, when I asked him, but later, he opened up to me about how much it meant to him that I had at least thought of him enough to even ask.

One study estimated that the risk of divorce was 22 percent higher among couples that suffered a miscarriage or stillbirth (Robert Wood Johnson Foundation 2020). I'm not sharing that fact to scare you or make you question your relationship or worry that you'll become part of the statistic. I share this to show you why it's so important to talk about grief and how you and your partner both process it. Knowing this can help tremendously in maintaining open and effective lines of communication in your relationship. My best advice is to listen. Take the time to listen to your partner. Don't push them to open up faster than they're ready. Remember that every person processes grief differently and will take the path to healing in their own way. Just do your best to be a loving partner and walk alongside them for the journey.

CHAPTER FOUR

THE IN-BETWEEN AND INDEX CARDS

"I am with you and will watch over you wherever you
go, and I will bring you back to this land. I will not
leave you until I have done what I have promised you."
—Genesis 28:15

I N THE TIME BETWEEN OUR FIRST AND SECOND ULTRASOUND, IT
felt like my whole world had come to a stop. Not the world
outside me, just *my* world. It was like everything around me was
moving in fast-forward, and I was just standing there in the middle. Still. Silent. Numb. And all of the bodies around me began
to move so fast that their motions became colorful blurred lines
surrounding my weary body.

On a Wednesday, exactly one week after our first ultrasound,
we went to the OB office again. I had been praying for a week
straight for a miracle, a misunderstanding, a baby that was hidden
in my belly. Hoping they just couldn't find the little cutie the first
time. I reclined back in the same tan leather chair with the crinkly
paper. We waited. The ultrasound technician spoke. Nothing had
changed. The same blonde lady with the same perky bun gave us
the same devastating news she had given us the week before . . .

How? I thought. I had prayed for a miracle. I thought my story was supposed to end with a *miracle*. I thought this was God's chance to show up for me in a way that was supernatural. I was hoping to leave that doctor's office with a long sheet of ultrasound pictures. But I didn't. I expected them to tell me they missed something. But they didn't.

The harshest part of it all was that after that second ultrasound, we had confirmation of a miscarriage, but my body still had absolutely no idea. My hCG levels were still rising (which they do in a normal pregnancy), and my body hadn't started bleeding yet. I was on a cruel hamster wheel of confusion and devastation. We didn't know why this had happened. We didn't know if it had implications for future pregnancies. We didn't know why I was showing that I had a miscarriage on a scan but not physically in my body. We didn't know why the baby stopped growing so soon after conception. Yet here I was, nine weeks along, and my body was still nurturing the pregnancy as if it were viable.

On the one hand, we finally had concrete answers. On the other hand, we still knew nothing at all. I wanted to be out of the waiting season. I wanted to have the baby or not have the baby at this point. The middle was just too painful. The not knowing was awful.

My OB called us at home a few hours later, after she had had time to review my ultrasound, and confirmed that it was a miscarriage. She offered to prescribe me some medicine to help me pass the baby at home since the loss was already inevitable. I politely declined. Looking back now, I wonder if I declined because of my moral beliefs or because I still had those women's stories from the forum in my head about it all having been a huge mistake. Perhaps both? I thought that maybe two ultrasounds weren't enough. I thought that maybe there was still some hope somehow. I heard what the doctors said, and I wasn't in complete denial. But since my body wasn't actually physically miscarrying yet on its own, I had to wonder why. That teeny percentage, that small little chance that they were wrong, was enough for me to prolong this middle that I wanted so badly to be over.

In the days that followed, I couldn't think about anything else. I was consumed with researching and trying to control or "fix" my situation. Even when I knew there was no control, I wanted to find something that would give me a little sliver of hope. I just wanted some form of evidence that said I wasn't crazy for still believing in a miracle. After all, God isn't called the God of miracles for nothing, right? I've seen Him perform miracles in so many of the lives of the people I love, so why not mine?

At that time, my perspective and priorities drastically changed. I had to count my blessings daily and remind myself of what I did have. I had to consciously switch my focus to gratitude. And it was hard to do.

* * *

It was November 7, 2020, about ten days after my initial ultrasound, and it was an oddly warm fall day in Michigan. It was 70-something degrees, which never happens for us that late in the year. We took full advantage and spent the beautiful Saturday in the sunshine and got some fresh air. Years prior, a few of my friends had started an online Bible study on the book *It's Not Supposed to Be This Way* by Lysa TerKeurst. In it, TerKeurst takes readers on a journey to help them better process painful, unmet expectations. I hadn't read the book all the way through with them at the time, not because it wasn't good, but because I just wasn't in a season of my life where I thought I really needed that encouragement. But in the fall of 2020, given the circumstances I found myself in, I decided to pick it back up.

I climbed into the bed of my husband's truck and sat on the warm, black surface that lined it. (Is sitting in the bed of the truck and just hanging out in the yard a Mississippi thing? I think it is.) Then, I finally finished the book. I read the last line of the final chapter, closed the book, and jumped down out of the truck bed. I headed inside to go to the bathroom and noticed I had started bleeding. There it was—proof of what we feared the most. My body was finally miscarrying. I called my husband in from outside. We just hugged each other and cried. We were equally devastated and relieved. I know that sounds weird . . . but hear me out. We were devastated for obvious reasons. But the relief came from the simple fact that we didn't have to live in limbo anymore. We had been on this emotional roller coaster for ten days at that point, juggling being sad and trying to cope and heal and process with having hope and researching and praying for a miracle. It was all just too much. I was frustrated with my body for failing me and then frustrated all over again because it hadn't caught on yet to what all of us already knew. At that point, I was about ten weeks pregnant, and my body still had no idea that the baby had stopped growing months ago.

Derek and I hugged and cried right there in the mud room, just inside the garage door of our home. Our worst fears were confirmed, so we continued to weep. No one knew about our loss at this point except for close friends and family members. We got Chinese food for dinner and had a quiet movie night at home with just the two of us. Even though I started showing signs of a miscarriage that day, it would still be another week before I actually miscarried.

THE TWENTY-DAY DIFFERENCE

I took a picture of myself in the mirror when I was around seven weeks pregnant, before my first ultrasound. I was wearing light-blue overalls with a black, long-sleeved shirt. Looking back, my stomach barely even looked bloated, but I just couldn't wait to track my weekly and monthly bump pics. I was so excited to have a tiny human growing inside of me! It was about five days before the ultrasound that would alter the course of my life forever.

When I look at that picture, I envy that girl. She was so blissfully unaware of the pain she was about to experience. She had never gone through the heartbreak that was about to ensue. She didn't know what miscarriage felt like or what it was like to have to go back and untell your parents about your pregnancy. She had the next nine months to a year planned out and was picking out baby names and baby clothes. I used to envy that girl and how happy she was, mostly because there were moments during my miscarriage when I thought I was too far gone to ever become her again. Even though that's very much how I felt in that moment, I knew God's truth said otherwise. Deuteronomy 30:3 (The Message) says, "God, your God, will restore everything you lost; he'll have compassion on you; he'll come back and pick up the pieces from all the places where you were scattered." What a loving God; as infinite and big as He is, He would still take the time to help us pick up our broken pieces.

After my ultrasound, when we found out we were losing our precious baby, I wrote down several verses, including the one above, on bright blue and yellow index cards and taped them onto our bathroom mirror. I just wanted to have a louder voice in my head than the one that was telling me all sorts of lies about how I wasn't good enough, how this was somehow my fault, how I would never be a mom, and this was where my story "ended." No, I needed a voice that came from Jesus because those lies I was starting to actually believe were the voice of the enemy. A few of the other verses that I chose for my index cards were:

Isaiah 26:3: You will keep in perfect peace those whose minds are steadfast, because they trust in you.

Genesis 50:20: You intended to harm me, but God intended it for good to accomplish what is now being done, the saving of many lives.

1 Peter 5:10: And the God of all grace, who called you to his eternal glory in Christ, after you have suffered a little while, will Himself restore you and make you strong, firm and steadfast.

One night, after posting these index cards on my mirror, something happened. It was so small that I can't even recall what it was—but it was triggering. It instantly reminded me of my baby and the miscarriage. I started weeping in front of the kitchen sink, uttering words to my husband that he couldn't make out. I grabbed the dish towel and started uncontrollably sobbing into it. With desperation in my eyes, mascara running down my cheeks, and the hot water still running, I went to the bathroom to read my index cards and remind myself of the truth. Then I looked up and remembered the picture I had taken a few weeks before. So, I took another picture in the mirror. The next day, I posted the picture on Facebook next to the picture of me in my overalls, the one with my seven-week bloat of a baby bump. I posted the two pictures side by side with a caption:

The girl in the picture on the left stood in front of this mirror 21 days before that. She had the next nine months to a year planned out perfectly in her head. Just bought a cute newborn onesie and baby moccasins and was picking out her favorite baby names. So ready to show off that little bump, had forgotten every goal she had of a flat tummy or abs and couldn't find a pair of pants that fit . . . and was even thankful for it.

The girl in the picture to the right . . . stood here last night after sobbing uncontrollably into a dish towel at the kitchen sink without warning. Eyes red, swollen, and puffy in this picture, and the grief is almost too much to bear. And now surrounded by encouraging verses I taped to our mirror to remind myself who I am and whose I am.

Gosh, this road isn't easy, and I will never pretend it is. Some moments I feel at complete peace, and other moments the pain hits me like a mac truck. And with all the change that took place between these two pictures, complete night and day . . . I take heart in the fact that God never did. If you're walking this road, too, you're not alone. And there's a purpose in our pain.

"The Lord is close to the brokenhearted; He rescues those whose spirits are crushed." —Psalm 34:18

Romans 8:28 (NIV) says, "And we know that in all things God works for the good of those who love him, who have been called according to his purpose." Even on the hard days, especially on the hard days, reading those verses taped onto my bathroom mirror helped me to drown out the lies of the enemy. I was able to hear the voice of the Lord louder. I was reminded that the weapon may form, but it will not prosper. God used those little index cards to remind me that everything in my life works together for my good.

What's your version of index card reminders? What is it that reminds you of God's faithfulness? Maybe it actually is verses posted on your mirror. Or maybe it's just taking the time to watch the sunset. Maybe it's texting a close friend. Maybe it's diving deeper into the Word each morning. Whatever it is, find your "index cards," and be sure to look at them as often as you need to. They can be a great place to turn to when you're crying into the kitchen sink.

CHAPTER FIVE

SAFE SPACES AND FIXED GAZES

"Fixing our eyes on Jesus, the pioneer and
perfecter of faith." —Hebrews 12:2

O N A COLD, DREARY DAY IN EARLY NOVEMBER, MY HUSBAND and I felt just like the Michigan weather outside: isolated and desolate. Derek suggested we get out and do something fun— anything I wanted. So, I told him I wanted to go to T.J. Maxx because what girl doesn't love that store? Without hesitation, he agreed (told you he's amazing). We went into the store with no specific purpose, just to browse and get our minds off things. As we were walking past the clothing department to the back of the store where the home goods, decorations, and candles were, I realized that, for the first time in a long time, I had forgotten the pain I was in.

As we were smelling candles, my husband was making me laugh like he always does. He kept cracking jokes and trying on silly items or pointing out interesting décor to try and make me smile, and it was working. I was laughing so hard at one point that I wanted to take a video of whatever he was doing for my Instagram story. I grabbed my phone out of my back pocket, unlocked it, and opened up the app. Before I could even switch over to the camera to take the video, the first post on my timeline loaded. It was my childhood best friend's pregnancy announcement.

There was a post of a light-gray, cloth rocker with a teddy bear sitting on it with the caption "Baby coming soon! Due June 2021." My heart sank, and my stomach dropped. June would've been my due date too. I instantly broke out in a cold sweat. How could I not know about her pregnancy until now? How could I have found out this way? And of all the moments, why now? *We were having such a good time, and now everything is ruined,* I thought to myself.

Tears welled up in my eyes. My heart felt ripped open. Meanwhile, my husband had no idea what had just happened, so he was still cracking jokes in the background. I looked up at him with glazed-over eyes full of tears so large I could barely see more than a fuzzy outline of his face, and I said, "We have to leave. I want to go home." Completely and utterly confused, he reluctantly said, "Okay . . ." and we fast-walked silently back to the truck.

When my passenger door shut, I immediately burst into tears. With the patience he's known and loved for, Derek just sat there and waited on me. Finally, he whispered, "What on earth happened? Are you okay?" I explained to him what I'd seen. The pregnancy announcement. The shared due date. The ton of bricks I was just smacked over the head with. I just sat in the car and continued weeping.

I'm thankful for the safe space that is this book because if you've gone through the same loss I went through, I don't have to explain to you that my tears and sadness weren't because I wasn't happy for her. It wasn't me trying to be selfish in that moment and only think of myself. I don't have to explain to you that my breaking down wasn't because I didn't want to celebrate the precious life that my friend was growing. Because you get it. I'm sure you've experienced a similar pain where you were just going on about your life, trying for a few minutes to be anything but the woman who lost her baby, trying to have an ounce of normalcy back in your life, only to have it stripped away in a millisecond by something totally out of your control.

It stings down to your core's core. It's an emotional pain that you can physically feel. Even while I'm writing these words more than a year later, I still feel a tightness in my chest because this pain I'm describing was so familiar to me in that season. I remember it so well, and if this is still the season you're in, my friend, I want you to know that I see you. The people in the aisles at T.J. Maxx may not know or understand the hurt or pain you're going through as you fast-walk past them while holding back tears, your heart sunken deep into the pit of your stomach, but I do. The Lord sees you too, and He hasn't forgotten you.

When I was going through my miscarriage, and the wounds were still fresh, the Lord reminded me of His love in so many different ways. The CEO of my company and his wife sent me flowers as soon as they heard the news. Friends from Arizona sent us flowers and a gift card for a date night. I had an ice-cream cake delivered to my doorstep by a friend in Texas. My mom called me every single day to check on me and to talk about our days. Other friends bought me little devotionals for women who had lost their babies. Some of our dearest friends got me silver bangle bracelets that said, "I'll hold you in my heart until I can hold you in my arms." All of those moments were such tangible ways of God showing His love to me in that season, surrounding me with such an incredible community who loved me so well. They were the hands and feet of Jesus to me in that season.

GROUNDED IN TRUTH

The hardest part of my miscarriage for my friends and family was having to watch me go through the pain I was in. They didn't want to see me struggle the way I was. If you're like me, so many of the sweet, well-meaning people in your life just want to "fix" it. When I shared my grief with them, they would try so hard to counsel me, encourage me, and make it better. Their hearts were so pure, and I know they just wanted me to feel peace and security again. They wanted to help me heal. The people who love us don't want to see us in pain, but sometimes "fixing" isn't what we need. Sometimes, we just need to feel the pain and give honor to the baby that we lost by truly giving ourselves the space to grieve. So, can we create a safe space here to do that?

Let's just sit in the suck for a moment. We won't stay here, but let's get honest with ourselves and with God about our feelings. Pain is messy, so I won't tell you to move on or what your feelings and pain "should" or "shouldn't" look like. This is a judgment-free zone. So let it out. These feelings are so raw, so real. They're not truly understood by anyone who hasn't had to experience this specific heartbreak.

Here's what I want you to know: *you're not alone*. We're all trying to navigate being a member of this club that none of us asked to be a part of. It's okay to feel sad and angry. Feel those emotions. Your grief is real. The feeling that you've been robbed? I feel that too.

After my miscarriage, my emotions, logic, and reasoning were sometimes blurred and muddled. There were times I couldn't even identify the feelings I had in the moment. There's no right or wrong way to feel in this moment. Feel it all and feel it all at once.

Don't brush over the "bad" emotions so you can more quickly get to the "good" ones. It's *all* part of our process of healing.

I encourage you to also take away all "shoulds" and "shouldn'ts." Don't base your level of grief on how long you carried your child—the grief of someone who lost their child at five weeks isn't any easier than someone who lost their child at 25 weeks. We all weep the same, and a loss is a loss. It's hard, no matter what. Don't beat yourself up or compare your pain. Don't feel guilty for your own hurt just because you feel that someone else's loss is more extreme. I see you, and your hurt is valid.

After my miscarriage, I felt guilty for being happy, and I felt guilty for being sad. It seemed like everyone around me was sharing their pregnancy announcements on social media, and I was left with a broken heart and empty arms. I tried burying myself in work to forget what had happened and just get through it. I also tried taking things slow and listening to my body. Neither seemed to help.

I even felt embarrassed. At the time, I felt embarrassed that we had told so many people and had to untell them. Embarrassed about how easy it was for so many people's bodies to have kids while, for some reason, it wasn't for mine. Embarrassed that I still cried every few days because I "should be stronger than this." Even now, I fight the feelings of embarrassment that I still grieve the loss of something I never knew or had.

Our pain shouldn't have to be black and white. I've given myself permission to heal slowly and to heal quickly—to feel healed one day and have the wound completely re-opened the next, letting those emotions all flood back in at once. It's all okay. Being happy is okay, and so is being sad. Nehemiah 8:10 (NIV) says,

"The joy of the Lord is [our] strength." The joy of me, the joy of *you*, fails daily. My happiness is certainly fleeting with my circumstances, but when I fix my gaze on the joy that comes from the Lord, that's where I gain my strength, even on my hardest days.

I've talked to so many women who think feeling these emotions, being hurt and questioning, means they don't trust in God. They say things like, "I want a baby so badly, but I know that's wrong, and I should just be content with what I have." Contentment is absolutely important, but it's not that black and white. I think you can honor the Lord in your season of wanting more by being content with what you have but also by being honest with Him about your desires for your future. Having a hard time isn't a sin. We know that this grief is okay and even normal because Jesus experienced it. The Bible says in Isaiah 53:3 (BSB) that "[Jesus] was despised and rejected by men, a man of sorrows, acquainted with grief." He can sympathize with our emotions. The New Testament even records a time when Jesus wept after His friend Lazarus died (John 11:35 NIV).

When we model our suffering after Jesus, we're able to see the beautiful peace that can be found in the midst of our chaotic storms. When our minds beg us to forget the hurt, move on past this pain, and get over our suffering, we see that it's okay to weep. We don't have to rush past these feelings for fear of sinning or being ungrateful if we take a moment to be honest with ourselves and God.

Jesus wept (John 11:35 NIV, KJV). He was a man of sorrow and acquainted with grief, yes. But He also spent time alone with God. When we're hurt, such as when we sit in the suck, we need to be grounded in the truth of God's Word to make sure we don't stay there. Jesus, Son of God and equal to the Father in every way, spent time alone with Him on multiple occasions throughout the New Testament. When Jesus's cousin John the Baptist was beheaded, the Bible says, "When Jesus heard what had happened, he withdrew by boat privately to a solitary place" (Matt. 14:13 NIV). If the Son of God needs that time alone with God the Father, how much do *we* need that time alone with Him? This helps us sneak away from the chaos and the voices all around us offering different pieces of advice. We can bring our sorrow and offenses boldly before Him (Heb. 4:16 NIV) because He hears our prayers (Jer. 29:12–13 NIV). He desires to have a sense of community with us. He's a God who understands what pain feels like, and He wants to be the one we run to for healing.

Our friends and family, the encouraging books they give us (including this book), kind words, flowers, and even time cannot truly heal you. Those things are certainly helpful and welcomed, but only God can heal the deepest depths of our hearts. May we get honest with ourselves about our feelings and not rush too quickly past them. May we remember that God can sympathize with our weakness and our grief, especially on our hardest days. Let us sneak away with Him and spend time alone in His presence so that we can acknowledge our pain in a healthy way, grounded in the truth of God's Word.

"I have heard your prayer and seen your tears; I will heal you," God promises in 2 Kings 20:5 (NIV).

Let's allow Him to do so.

CHAPTER SIX

MIGHTY PRAYERS AND

HIDDEN MIRACLES

"Ask and you will receive, and your joy will be complete."
—John 16:24

E VERYTHING ABOUT THE PAIN FOLLOWING MY MISCARRIAGE
was hard. Even things I used to love became hard. Back in the
"good ole days," Friday used to signal the start of the weekend for
me, fun plans to go out with my husband and friends, and sleeping
in. It was my favorite day of the week. Then, when I got pregnant,
it became the day that started a new week in pregnancy. So, after
my miscarriage, I hated Fridays. I hated that constant reminder
of what I had lost. They were a reminder of the void that was ever
present in my heart and in my womb. They weren't fun anymore.
They were painful.

For so long after my miscarriage, I prayed that God would
just get me through Fridays, that they would sting a little less. I
prayed that I wouldn't dread Fridays or that, somehow, God would
help me forget what they stood for. I remember praying and asking
God for help when I hung out with my friends for the first time
since my miscarriage. I felt so embarrassed to be seen by them. We
had told them we were pregnant a few days before our first ultrasound, mostly because I have a big mouth and couldn't contain

my own excitement. So, when we lost the baby, I felt foolish. I felt dumb or silly for thinking we could really be pregnant or have the baby we told them about. Our friends were so supportive and caring and sent me thoughtful texts and prayed over us. It wasn't them who made me feel that way. It was just the enemy trying to fill me with guilt and shame so that I would separate myself from the people who were encouraging me the most.

Feeling so helpless and not even knowing where to start, I just asked God to help me get through this week, this day, even this minute that was set right before me. I prayed and asked God to help me get through the milestones of my former pregnancy, like the day when I would've been 20 weeks pregnant and halfway along or when we took Christmas pictures as a family with my niece and very pregnant sister-in-law who was due just six weeks before what would have been my due date. I continued asking God to get me through the little stuff.

I want you to know that those prayers matter to God. He cares so intimately about *every* detail of your life (Ps. 37:23 NIV). He wants to know about the tiniest things that trouble us. Sometimes I feel most loved when I'm praying for tiny little things in my days, inviting God to show up in the smallest of ways, and He does. It reminds me that as big as He is, He's also intimate. He's close, especially to the brokenhearted (Ps. 34:18 NIV). He desires communication and wants us to invite Him into our lives, minute by minute, and be fully reliant on Him.

But He's also a big God who can come through for us in more ways than just the tiny prayers we say to get through the day or the hour. One day, I felt the Lord challenge me in the midst of my small prayers to also pray big ones. As personal as those tiny prayers were, and as much as they mattered to God, I was praying for something way too small. It was as if I thought God was too small or His hand was too short to reach down into my story and truly do transformative work, so I prayed for the next few minutes to be easy instead.

The Bible says, "The prayer of a righteous person is powerful and effective" (James 5:16 NIV). There are so many stories in the Bible of people who prayed to God for huge things, and they saw God come through. One of my favorites is the story of when Elijah asked God to rain down fire from heaven in 1 Kings.

God tells Elijah to present himself to King Ahab, who had been hunting Elijah to have him killed. Ahab calls Elijah a troublemaker, but Elijah says that Ahab is the troublemaker because Ahab refused to obey God. He and his followers worship Baal and other false gods instead. Elijah tells Ahab to gather all of Israel and the prophets of the false gods at Mount Carmel, and he does.

When they get there, Elijah instructs the prophets of Baal, saying, "I am the only one of the Lord's prophets left, but Baal has four hundred and fifty prophets. Get two bulls for us. Let Baal's prophets choose one for themselves and let them cut it into pieces and put it on the wood but not set fire to it. I will prepare the other bull and put it on the wood but not set fire to it. Then, you call on the name of your god, and I will call on the name of the Lord. The god who answers by fire—he is God" (1 Kings 18:22–24 NIV).

Elijah used 12 stones to represent the 12 tribes of Israel and rebuilt the altar of the Lord. Then he did something the prophets of Baal didn't do; Elijah poured four large jugs of water over the bull and the wood he wanted to burn. He did this three times.

After that, Elijah dug a trench around the wood and the bull and filled it with three more jugs of water.

The prophets of Baal called on their god, but it, of course, didn't answer. After hours of waiting, Elijah finally called on God:

> *"Lord, the God of Abraham, Isaac and Israel, let it be known today that you are God in Israel and that I am your servant and have done all these things at your command. Answer me, Lord, answer me, so these people will know that you, Lord, are God, and that you are turning their hearts back again." Then the fire of the Lord fell and burned up the sacrifice, the wood, the stones and the soil, and also licked up the water in the trench. (1 Kings 18:36–38 NIV)*

What an amazing testament to God's power and faithfulness! I mean, this is a massive picture of God's ability and strength. The fire of the Lord burned up not only the wet bull and wet wood but also the water and even the stones from the altar! Elijah not only prayed that God would burn up the bull by raining fire down from heaven, but he also made it scientifically impossible to burn by wetting the entire pile. Even the stones burned! This is a huge ask of God by Elijah, and He came through for Elijah the same way He desires to come through for us in our times of hurt.

In Joshua 10:12–14 (NIV), we see God's vast power and another huge, bold prayer:

> *On the day the Lord gave the Amorites over to Israel, Joshua said to the Lord in the presence of Israel: "Sun, stand still over Gibeon, and you, moon, over the Valley of Aijalon." So the*

sun stood still, and the moon stopped, till the nation avenged itself on its enemies, as it is written in the Book of Jashar. The sun stopped in the middle of the sky and delayed going down about a full day. There has never been a day like it before or since, a day when the Lord listened to a human being. Surely the Lord was fighting for Israel!

God literally created the sun, and even it has to obey Him. So, why was I dumbing down my prayers to fit what I thought God was capable of? Was it because I didn't think He was able to hear me or accomplish more than what little I was asking Him for? Was it because I was afraid He wouldn't answer my prayers the way I wanted Him to? Was I trying to keep my faith intact by asking God for things I knew He *could* and *would* "come through" on? Maybe I was afraid that if I prayed to God for the bigger things I knew He *could* do but might *not* do, my faith would've been rattled.

After our first ultrasound, I prayed for a miracle. I asked God to show His glory at our next ultrasound and for the ultrasound tech to find the heartbeat of a healthy baby! That didn't happen.

Before that second ultrasound, I had prepared for the worst. But in my heart of hearts, I knew God's power. I knew that He could perform this miracle if He chose to, so why didn't He? Why was I left with so many unanswered questions? The reason for my loss was, "This just happens sometimes." No closure. No heartbeat. No miracle. Just a positive pregnancy test, an empty sac, and a broken heart. I prayed. I wept. I mourned and pleaded for a miracle. And I didn't get my miracle.

CHANGED PRAYERS AND CHANGED HEARTS

So, what do we do when we pray big (or small) prayers and God doesn't answer them in the way we think He should? When the wires seemingly get crossed? How can we trust that He is still good or that He even hears us? These were the questions that shook me to my core and echoed in my mind for weeks. I wanted to pray bigger prayers, but what did that look like? And what if I prayed those big prayers and God didn't deliver on them? Then what? What should I even pray for or ask God for? What's prayer really for? What's prayer really all about?

Hebrews 4:14–16 (English Standard Version) tells us, "Since then we have a great high priest who has passed through the heavens, Jesus, the Son of God, let us hold fast our confession. For we do not have a high priest who is unable to sympathize with our weaknesses, but one who in every respect has been tempted as we are, yet without sin. Let us then with confidence draw near to the throne of grace, that we may receive mercy and find grace to help in time of need." If we continue reading, Hebrews 6:19 (NIV) says, "We have this hope as an anchor for the soul, firm and secure." When we pray, we're praying to a high priest who's able to sympathize with our weaknesses. We can confidently and boldly come before Him to receive grace and mercy. That's the gift of prayer—grace and mercy. So, when we're going through trials in our life and come before God with them, we can expect to receive grace and mercy from Him for the season we're in, whether our situation changes or not. Prayer isn't a transactional encounter with God in which we pray for anything we want, and He gives it to us. In his book *Follow Me*, pastor and author David Platt says, "The primary purpose of prayer is not to get something, but to know Someone"

(Platt 2013). The prize for our prayers isn't always getting more of what we *want* but getting more of *who* we need most.

We can't manipulate God into giving us what we want with our prayers. "The function of prayer is not to influence God but rather to change the nature of the one who prays," Soren Kierkegaard wrote (Kierkegaard 1938). The same idea has also been put this way in the film *Shadowlands*, based on C.S. Lewis's life: "Prayer doesn't change God; it changes me" (Attenborough 1993). The point of prayer isn't to tell God what we need as though to enlighten Him to our needs. He already knows our needs (Mat. 6:8 NIV). It's also not to tell Him our desires or requests; He knows those as well. When we pray, we communicate with God and receive His grace, His mercy, and ultimately, more of Him. When our prayers are heard by God but not answered the way we wanted them to be, we have grown in our faith and reached a place where we have gotten to know the character and heart of God more deeply through our prayer life so that we trust His plan and His choosing of the outcome. "When the opposite of your prayer occurs, your prayer hasn't been ignored; it's been considered and refused for your ultimate good," C.S. Lewis reminds us (AZQuotes.com).

We know that prayer is important. The Bible speaks about prayer over 600 times. Charles Spurgeon even says, "As well could you expect a plant to grow without air and water as to expect your heart to grow without prayer and faith" (Spurgeon 1859).

I get it. Maybe you haven't bought into the whole idea of faith yet. That's okay! This book is for you too, and so are the fundamental principles in it. Maybe you don't know much about God and don't have a personal relationship with Him yet. That would make this foundation of faith a hard one for you to stand on when thinking about the importance of prayer. So, let's look at a few of the physiological scientific benefits of prayer as well.

Harold G. Koenig is a psychiatrist and a faculty member of the Center for Spirituality, Theology and Health at Duke University. In his book *The Healing Power of Faith*, he tells us about the physiological benefits of prayer and how it can help you triumph over disease (Koenig 2001). Although miscarriage isn't a disease, the principles are the same. Koenig notes how prayer can help relieve stress. In times of intense grief, it's common to feel alone. Prayer can help alleviate that feeling of loneliness. Believing that God is listening to your prayers takes you out of isolation. Koenig also cites the power of gratitude through prayer (Koenig 2001). Praying can make you more aware of and more thankful for your present moment and the blessings it holds.

Scientifically speaking, prayer elicits a relaxation response, which lowers blood pressure and other factors heightened by stress (Sloan et al. 2003). It can enhance a person's hopes and expectations, and that, in turn, can positively impact health. Prayer can also bring about feelings of gratitude, compassion, forgiveness, and hope, all of which are associated with healing and wellness (Portelli 2016).

Overall, prayer can help you create a more positive and hopeful worldview. All of these positive mental changes can lead to positive physical changes. In that way, prayer is both a spiritual and a physical exercise that can carry us through difficult seasons.

A DIFFERENT MIRACLE

In my own journey, I learned to accept God's choice and His authority in my life to allow this miscarriage to happen. I know He didn't cause this or choose this pain for me. But because there's sin in the world, there's also pain (Gen. 3 NIV). And since I remembered God's promise to me was to use my pain and that I wouldn't have to endure this pain for nothing, my choice was to trust Him. He's made that same promise to all who put their trust in Him—the promise that He "works all things together for the good of those who love Him, who are called according to His purpose" (Rom. 8:28 BSB). My choice was to still see His goodness in the midst of the hardest season I've ever had to walk through. I clung to the verse that I had found right after my ultrasound, Genesis 28:15 (NIV): "I am with you and will watch over you wherever you go, and I will bring you back to this land. I will not leave you until I have done what I have promised you."

In choosing to trust God's goodness, I shifted my question from *why* didn't you give me the miracle I begged for to *what do you want me to learn from this?* He showed me that my opportunity to pray big prayers wasn't over just because I didn't get my miracle the first time. So, I began to pray for a miracle again, but this time, I asked Him for a different miracle. Miscarriage will always be a part of my story. But I didn't want anxiety, fear, depression, bitterness, resentment, anger, or worry to be my story. So, my bold, audacious prayers became focused on praying against each of those things.

I knew God wanted to heal my heart, but He also wanted me to ask Him for healing. He wanted me to trust that He still listened to me and desired to do just that. I prayed against anxiety and the fear that I would never be able to have another healthy pregnancy. I prayed against depression, especially since I had my miscarriage in winter during a global pandemic. I prayed against bitterness toward women who were pregnant.

I know that may sound harsh, but again, this book is a safe space, and that was my reality. It seemed like everyone was posting pregnancy announcements on social media. My newsfeed was flooded with ultrasound pictures, wide grins, and comments of congratulations.

When my flesh begged me to choose bitterness, I prayed that God would soften my heart so I could genuinely be happy for all of my pregnant friends and acquaintances. I didn't want to feel resentment toward God or my body for "failing me" (as I felt it had) and allowing this to happen. I also prayed against worry. I was worried that I wouldn't be able to get pregnant again, and part of me was worried that I would. Then what? How would I deal with pregnancy after a loss like this one? I was terrified of either outcome.

1 John 5:14 (ESV) tells us, "And this is the confidence that we have toward him, that if we ask anything according to his will he hears us." God desires that we stand boldly before Him with our audacious prayers. He wants to display His glory through us. One way He can do that is by answering big, specific prayers.

To echo God's own challenge to me, what are the things you should *really* be praying for? In what areas do you feel called to submit to God's authority and how He will or has answered your prayers? What emotions have you been holding onto that aren't from the Lord that you need to release? Maybe it's anger or bitterness. Maybe it's anxiety or resentment. What prayers have you been praying that are too small? What big, bold prayers can you begin to pray so that you can give God the opportunity to put His glory on display in your life for everyone to see?

CHAPTER SEVEN

GROCERY STORES AND GRAY AREAS

"'For I know the plans I have for you,' declares the Lord,
'plans to prosper you and not to harm you, plans to give
you hope and a future.'" —Jeremiah 29:11

A LITTLE WHILE AFTER LEARNING OF MY MISCARRIAGE, I WAS IN the grocery store pushing a shopping cart and looking at nutrition labels when I heard a little kid laughing. I looked up from the box of protein bars I was holding to see a mom with a messy bun, a toddler at her side, and a younger child seated in the front of the cart with her little legs dangling down. They were all talking with one another, the children mostly bickering back and forth. They were begging their mom to buy a box of fruit snacks. The mom was holding a paper coffee cup with a familiar white and green logo. Her baggy t-shirt had a slobber or spit-up stain on it. When she turned to the side to grab another item off the shelf, I saw a half-smile and heard a gentle "no, we don't need any more of that" spoken to her son. She looked tired, but she looked happy. I wanted that. I wanted the middle-of-the-night wake-ups, the poopy diapers, the spit-up on my clothes, the tired eyes and disheveled hair. I was happy to have it all. It'd be proof I was a mom, which I wanted more than anything.

A little later, I was standing in the aisle filled with chips and snack foods, and a college-aged girl with dark-brown hair pulled back in a single braid walked past me. Her friend later joined her. I overheard bits of a conversation about their plans for that weekend and a basketball game they were attending. I remembered those days, though they felt like an entire lifetime ago. So much had changed since then—my marital status, priorities, perspective. For so many years, my life was all about weekend plans and spending as much time with my friends as humanly possible.

After deciding on my box of snack bars and dropping it into my half-full cart, it dawned on me: I didn't fit in with any of them, none of the people I had just passed in the aisle. I wasn't a mom yet, like the woman with her children, but I couldn't relate to anyone who wasn't a mom either. I had never done any of the "mom" things before. I never had the chance to. But I did have the next few years planned out in my head. The plans weren't for the party happening that weekend or the basketball game I'd be going to with a group of friends in between studying sessions. My plans were so different now. I had planned out family pictures, thinking about the first time our baby would talk, crawl, walk. I imagined my husband becoming a baseball or soccer coach. It was all planned. Then it was all ripped out from underneath me.

Truthfully, I was a mom. I knew that. But as both of those women walked past me in the aisle that day, they didn't know that. I didn't have a baby in a car seat or a child holding my hand. I didn't have a baby bump to prove I was a mom. I found myself trapped in a gray area. I felt like I didn't know who I was anymore, and certainly, no one else knew who I was. I was in the middle, in the in-between. A mom but also not a mom. What a weird place to be . . . It was like a desert, desolate and isolated. Pain is definitely messy. So is the journey we're on. But we're moving forward on this path of healing. On the other side of pain, the pain we can't see past in this moment, there's a promise waiting for us. But first, we must move through this gray area. And unless you've had to experience it, you can never truly comprehend the depths of loneliness that await you in that gray area. Or a grocery store.

Maybe your story is different. Maybe your gray area looks different than mine. Maybe you already have a child. Maybe your hard question is, "How many kids do you have?" How do we answer that? Do we just say the number that are standing before us and leave out someone special who can't be with us physically? Or do we include our angel in the count and hope the other person doesn't ask questions? Do we try to explain what happened in 30 seconds or less to a well-meaning stranger who was just trying to make small talk?

A mom but not a mom was where I found myself. I couldn't be both, could I? In that blurry desert season, I had to learn to accept that this was where I was for the time being. There was no black and white. It was gray. There was no clarity; it was all blurry. There was no one around me who could understand; it was a desert. *And* an island. It was a deserted island, and I was Tom Hanks, without even Wilson to keep me company. I had to learn to be okay with the in-between. I had to get comfortable with the "already, but not yet" space. I had to come to terms with the fact that I wouldn't have all the answers yet, if ever. I had to learn to live with my emotions, something that's extremely hard for me to do. I'd much rather move past the hard feelings and on to something happier to mask the pain. This desert forced me to sit for a while in my emotions so that I could identify them and begin to cope with the pain. I remembered what God had told me, that this would be used for my good. I had to have faith during the gray blur that was my life—that His promise remained. God hadn't changed His Word or His mind just because I couldn't see His promise fulfilled yet.

HAPPINESS OR JOY?

In this season of my life, I learned so much about joy. And I learned the difference between happiness and joy. Happiness is fleeting. It's based on our circumstances and how we feel. But joy is a state of being. It's a "fruit of the Spirit" (Gal. 5:22 NIV) that we have complete access to at all times as children of God, no matter what's going on around us. It was something that was especially important for me to access in this stuck-in-the-middle season.

I love personality tests (anyone else?), and someone a few years ago encouraged me to take the StrengthsFinder test, a personal development tool created by Gallup Education that helps individuals realize their greatest strengths. I wasn't surprised at all when, at the top of the list of my five greatest strengths, it said "futuristic." That's me. I'm very good at visualizing the future, knowing what I want, and then taking the action steps to get there. It's a great strength, my best strength, apparently. But every strength can also be our greatest weakness if we don't use it properly. One of my biggest downfalls in being futuristic is that it's hard for me to just be present in the moment without thinking of what comes next or what I could be doing instead. I struggle with contentment and happiness in the place I'm in. I'm always chasing the next best thing, especially when I'm not actively seeking God in my life.

When I'm in tune with the Lord and spend time with Him daily, I'm more aligned with Him and satisfied with where I'm at. That doesn't mean I'm perfect or that I can't strive for more or work to become my best. It simply means that I access the joy that He offers me freely, right where I'm at. When I chase happiness, I think it can't be found where I'm at right now, so I need to quickly move on to the next best thing to find it. Or when my situation all around me doesn't look "good," then I'm not happy because happiness is based on what's going on around us. When we're on vacation or when we lose two pounds or when we're getting along with our spouse, we're happy. But what happens when things aren't going our way?

After I had my miscarriage, it became obvious to me that happiness and joy were totally separate. And in those days and months that followed, I felt like I lived out the difference. Of course, I wasn't happy with what happened to me. Of course, I wasn't happy that I had lost my baby or that my body was going through painful changes. But I still had joy. I know; it was weird to me too. For me, the joy that I had during that season looked like having peace in knowing that God was still there and hadn't left me, even when I was bawling my eyes out at the kitchen sink. It looked like seeing Him in the little things throughout my day, like a phone call from a friend to cheer me up. Joy during my miscarriage was possible because I knew this wouldn't be my home forever. I know that this is all temporary and that when I die, I'm going to heaven where there are no tears, no pain, no sorrow, no miscarriage. When I viewed my situation in light of eternity, I understood what Paul was talking about when He said, "For this light momentary affliction is preparing for us an eternal weight of glory beyond all comparison" (2 Cor. 4:17 ESV).

I could have joy even when I wasn't happy. I didn't have to wait for my circumstances to change to have good days. The truth I've learned is that I can find joy in the Lord where I'm at *now*—in the midst of my pain, grief, and heartache of miscarriage. If I were to have a baby, I wouldn't automatically have joy in the Lord. Having a baby would make me happier than I was during my miscarriage, of course. But we're talking about *joy*. And joy is a choice. We can choose to access it through the Holy Spirit if we know Jesus as our Savior, or we can choose not to. Joy is readily available to us even now as we're suffering, but He won't force it upon us. We must choose joy to have hope in the hard times and to see Him as the source of our blessings in the good times.

Psalm 16:11 (ESV) says, "You make known to me the path of life; in your presence there is fullness of joy; at your right hand are pleasures forevermore." Having "fullness of joy" is what I want to be known for. I don't want to be the person who's constantly running (in vain) after the next best thing to find her happiness. I don't want to be the woman who dodges situations or emotions that are uncomfortable for the sake of my happiness. I want to be known for being the woman who found joy, contentment, and satisfaction in the Lord even during the lowest points of my life. Don't you?

A CHOSEN PEOPLE

The gray area, this in-between, also forced me, in a way, to find my identity and hope not in motherhood but in Christ for true satisfaction. It forced me to dig deep into who I truly was and what God says about me.

Did you know that Satan loves to try and get us to believe lies about ourselves? He loves to make us believe we're less than, inadequate, weak, ugly, victims, unlovable, unwanted, and ashamed. Satan would love for us to believe that we don't belong. Because as long as we can believe those lies about ourselves, we'll never fully step into the role of who God truly created us to be.

The enemy loves to twist what God says about us so that we base who we are on how we feel or on our circumstances instead. But the Bible says in 1 Peter 2:9 (NIV), "But you are a chosen people, a royal priesthood, a holy nation, God's special possession, that you may declare the praises of him who called you out of darkness into his wonderful light."

I'm just curious how much would change about us if we constantly showed up like a chosen people, like royalty. I don't know about you, but I'd walk a little straighter with my head held higher. Even on our worst days, we're still loved and favored by God. I pray that we can truly believe that. I pray we don't believe what culture or society says about us. I pray that our worth, our value, and our identity aren't measured by the world and its standards but that we believe what God's Word says is true of us.

Identity is so important to God, so much so that He created us in His image (Genesis 1:27 NIV). Even when our circumstances beg us to believe otherwise, I pray that we see ourselves the way God sees us, not any better and not any less.

I pray that motherhood doesn't define us. Regardless of whether or not I have a child, I can find my identity in being a child of God (John 1:12 NIV). I hope that you don't think any less of yourself for losing a baby or multiple babies and that you don't begin to define yourself as someone who has to carry the weight of that struggle around every day. I pray that you won't see yourself as less than because you're not a mom.

My prayer is that we can firmly place our worth and identity in Him and who He says we are, not the blessing we pray to receive or the woman we hope to become, because when we believe that what God says about us is true, we'll see His blessings begin to explode in our lives. We'll begin to see His goodness show up in the middle of where we are, right in this moment—*before* we get where we're going. And when we see God show up for us just as we are, we'll be reminded that He's not waiting on us to change or become something better or different. He accepts us.

LACKING NOTHING

We don't serve a God who's absent during our desert seasons. I know it feels lonely, but I promise God is there every step of the way. If you're familiar with the story in the Bible of the Israelites leaving Egypt to enter the Promised Land, you know that they're God's chosen people. He led them out of slavery in Egypt by sending ten plagues so that Pharaoh would let them go (Exod. 7–11 NIV). After Pharaoh finally let the Israelites out of his captivity, God led them through the Red Sea by parting the waters (Exod. 14 NIV). God wanted to take them from Egypt into the Promised Land of Canaan. But there were times on the way to Canaan when the Israelites grumbled and complained, doubted God, and refused to enter the Promised Land. They feared their enemies more than they trusted God. So, God punished them by making them wander in the wilderness for 40 years until they trusted and obeyed Him. While they were in the desert those 40 years, the Israelites lacked faith, disobeyed, and worshipped false gods.

Even though the Israelites disobeyed and worshipped false gods, God still provided for them. He sent them *literal* food from heaven and kept them safe. In Deuteronomy 29:5 (NIV), God says, "During the forty years that I led you through the wilderness, your clothes did not wear out, nor did the sandals on your feet."

Even though the Israelites' journey wasn't a straight line from Egypt to the Promised Land, God remained with them and led them every step of the way. God is such a personal God and cares about us and for us, right down to our shoes. He's not there at a distance or watching from afar. He's a near, close God who guides us like He guided the Israelites day and night, filling our tummies and sustaining the soles of our shoes. Because that's how deeply and intimately He cares for us too.

I still remember times when, right after losing our baby, I would be having a hard day, and He would bring me to someone's mind. They would randomly text me and tell me they were thinking of me, or my mom would call and check on me. He provided rest for me when I was bedridden for two weeks after my miscarriage. I could've chosen to see what happened in each of those moments as coincidences. I could've viewed being bedridden as a setback. But I chose to view them as God's winks. They were God's little blessings and favors in my life. They were all tangible ways He was still providing for me in my desert season.

But it's easy to forget that God provides, even right after He does it. We ask God to provide for us. He shows up. We praise Him. Then something else happens in our lives, we panic, and we forget all over again that He's still our Provider, just like the Israelites did. When the Israelites were wandering in the desert, they sometimes forgot that the Lord provided for them. In Exodus 17 (NIV), they began arguing with Moses about how thirsty they were. They feared they would die of thirst. Then God ordered

Moses to strike a rock, and out poured enough water for all the Israelites. This story reminds us that even the most cared-for people can forget God's goodness and try to put Him to the test.

This all happened *after* the Lord provided a cloud during the day and a fire by night to guide them. This was *after* they saw God part the Red Sea, and they walked through it on dry land and saw their enemies swallowed up in the ocean behind them when God brought the waters back together. This was *after* He provided manna for them to eat by raining it down from the sky. Yet, they were still so quick to complain and worry that God couldn't or wouldn't provide something as small as water for them. Even still, God, in His gracious patience, provided for them.

Trusting God in the midst of our desert is hard. The waiting is tough, and it's easier to see the lack on most days. Having faith in the in-between, where we've received a promise but haven't yet seen it come to pass, is tough work. In Deuteronomy 2:7 (ESV), we're reminded that our needs are all met even in this desert season, just like the Israelites' needs were met. It says, "For the Lord your God has blessed you in all the work of your hands. He knows you are going through this great wilderness. These forty years the Lord your God has been with you. You have lacked nothing."

God was faithful then, and He is faithful now. Even in the desert, His people *lacked nothing.* What hope! We may be in a time of isolation—the gray and blurry middle—mentally, emotionally, and maybe even spiritually. But lacking nothing—that's our state. We may not have everything we want—me writing this book and you reading it is proof that we've gone through tough, painful things—but He has truly provided everything we needed along the way. He's the same God as He was yesterday and will be today and forever. Knowing that, we can trust that God will continue to provide for us in our desert season, the same way He always has.

Just like with the Israelites, God is leading us to our Promised Land, the place where we'll see how this will all be used for good. He's providing for us even in these moments when our journey is tough and when circumstances don't look the way we thought they would. The Promised Land is still where we're headed. When we arrive, we'll do so with everything we've ever needed, provided by a God who *is* provision. It's His character. He can't *not* provide for us. Provision is who He is. After passing through this in-between space, we'll arrive safely into the arms of our promise, completely taken care of.

FAITHFUL REMINDERS

From a zoomed-out aerial view, we may see the Israelites as foolish for forgetting so quickly that God had always been there for them. But don't we do the same thing? We know how the story of the Israelites in the desert ends. We can scan to the next chapter to see the outcome, but they couldn't. Wouldn't it be easier if we could just skim to the next chapter of our desert season and read what will happen next? But we can't, and that's where faith comes in. The key to having faith in our current moment is remembering God's past faithfulness. When we consider the ways in which He's shown up for us in our past, it helps us create a foundation of trust in Him and believe that He's also going to be faithful in our future.

The key to surviving the middle, where nothing makes sense, is remembering God's past faithfulness. That's what the Israelites did just before they arrived at Jericho before entering the Promised Land. In Joshua 4, they set up stones to remind them of God's faithfulness and how He'd always been with them.

When I went through my miscarriage, I set up my own stones to remind myself of the times God provided for me.

He was there in 2011 when my parents went through a nasty divorce. That year, He protected my dad from almost taking his own life. I remembered how He protected my mom, my brother, and me by sending Godly men from our church into our lives to step in and love and encourage us. When we didn't feel safe, they would come to our home and sit with us. I know He saved me emotionally by helping me forget a lot of the hurtful details. He left just enough memories there for me to use as a testimony of His goodness.

Then, because I was seeking the Lord so closely at the time, I decided I wanted to forgo college for a year. Instead, I decided to travel with a ministry team around the country for a year as a children's pastor. Then, while I was with that ministry team, He set up the opportunity for me to share my story of forgiveness toward my dad in front of thousands of women at conferences we went to. Through that experience, God was even faithful by helping me rebuild my relationship with my dad.

I ended up moving to one of the cities we visited that year on the road. I started school there, and when I changed jobs, I met Derek. Looking back, I see that everything lined up perfectly for me to meet my husband. Had my parents not gone through their divorce, I may not have sought the Lord so diligently. Had I not traveled with the ministry team, I never would've known about the town that I'm living in today in West Michigan.

My parents' divorce was, at that point, the hardest thing I had ever gone through. But I see now that God was matching me step for step. He was faithful the whole time and never let me drown under the waves that sometimes felt crushing. He always took care of me, and He even used that pain to bring about some of the biggest blessings of my life. I see now that all of it was good. Reminding myself of these painful moments in my life when God showed up helped me have faith that He'd do it again. When we remember God's past faithfulness to us, it helps to remind us that we can trust Him in the present, that He came through for us before, and He'll do it again.

The evidence of the Lord's faithfulness to the Israelites is a testimony to our future generations. As we set up our own stones, let's remember to tell our future children and our children's children how God has always shown up for us. Just as He did with the Israelites, and just as He does for us, He'll do it for them. As Hebrews 13:8 (NIV) reminds us, "Jesus Christ is the same yesterday and today and forever."

What are some of the things the Lord has done for you in your life so far? What stones do you need to lay down as a reminder of His past faithfulness? How will this help you lean into Him and trust Him during the in-between, the desert season? How will remembering his faithfulness to you even now help you in times of healing from grief in the future?

CHAPTER EIGHT

THE PREPARATION AND THE PROMISE

"We also glory in our sufferings, because we know that
suffering produces perseverance; perseverance, character;
and character, hope." —Romans 5:3–4

JUST BECAUSE THE JOURNEY LOOKS DIFFERENT THAN WE
thought it would doesn't mean the destination has changed or
that God forgot His promises to us. In fact, He's using this journey
on the way to our destination to shape us into who we need to be.
This is crucial to making sure that when we get to the destination,
we're prepared to take claim of His promise over our life.

During the Israelites' time in the desert, not only did God
provide for them, but He also grew their character. We know this
because the Bible says, "The Lord your God led you all the way in
the wilderness these forty years, to humble and test you in order to
know what was in your heart, whether or not you would keep His
commands" (Deut. 8:2 NIV). God knew the Promised Land He
had waiting for them would require a different, better version of
them. And He used their time in the desert to create that version
of them, to build their character, and to make them more like Him.
His purpose was to grow them enough so they could not only *ob-
tain* but also *sustain* the blessing that He was walking them into.

He does the same for us in our desert season. God wants to make sure that our character, too, is strong enough to sustain the blessing He's bringing us into. I'm not saying God sentenced you to the situation you're in now to teach you a lesson. But He will use these times of hurt, pain, loneliness, and grief to grow and prepare us for the blessing He's promised that's waiting for us just up ahead. His desire isn't that we'll just receive the blessing but that we'll also have the posture and maturity to *sustain* the blessing too.

In my own desert, God creates the character within me to sustain the blessings I'm asking Him for. He wants to make me more like Him, and to do that, He must grow my character *before* giving me the blessing He's promised. Something I pray often is, "God, don't let my blessings take me further than my character can sustain me."

Even though your desert is a detour, God is still with you, and there's purpose here. He's calling you higher, to the next level, to the version of you that's required for the promise you're about to step into.

THE BREAKING BEFORE THE BLESSING

The desert isn't our destination, and the heartbreak we experience isn't the end of our story. It's actually the setup for it. By taking us through a desert season, where we're solely dependent upon Him, God's able to chip away at our own selfish desires and tendencies. As we rid ourselves of pieces of us that are holding us back from who God's calling us to be, there's more room for Him. The character building, the breaking off of pieces of our own fleshly desires, creates a platform for Him to display His glory. This is where the purpose of our pain comes in. This is often when and where the Lord reveals our destiny.

Our breaking isn't meant to ruin us—just the opposite. It's the prerequisite for our blessing. One of my favorite stories in the Bible is the story of the five loaves and two fish. It can be found in all four of the Gospels (Matthew, Mark, Luke, and John), but I'll use some excerpts from Matthew's and Luke's versions. Matthew 14:13–21 (ESV) tells us the story:

> *Now when Jesus heard this, he withdrew from there in a boat to a desolate place by himself. But when the crowds heard it, they followed him on foot from the towns. When he went ashore he saw a great crowd, and he had compassion on them and healed their sick. Now when it was evening, the disciples came to him and said, "This is a desolate place, and the day is now over; send the crowds away to go into the villages and buy food for themselves." But Jesus said, "They need not go away; you give them something to eat." They said to him, "We have only five loaves here and two fish." And he said, "Bring them here to me." Then he ordered the crowds to sit down on the grass, and taking the five loaves and the two fish, he looked up to heaven and said a blessing. Then he broke the loaves and gave them to the disciples, and the disciples gave them to the crowds. And they all ate and were satisfied. And they took up twelve baskets full of the broken pieces left over. And those who ate were about five thousand men, besides women and children.*

What we learn about Jesus from this story is that He has a compassionate heart toward people. Just when the disciples were ready to leave the crowd of people to be alone (rightfully so—

they'd been ministering to a crowd with Jesus all day), Jesus saw the needs of the crowd and decided to stay. Jesus isn't in a hurry to move past our needs; He's willing and ready to provide what we need at just the right time. He's never too tired to take care of us, never too busy to notice what we need.

Luke 9:16 (ESV) says, "He looked up to heaven and said a blessing." Before He performed the miracle and before He gave the people their blessing, Jesus looked up to heaven. He turned His face toward the Provider. He didn't focus on what He lacked or the need that was all around Him. He didn't focus on the crowd that was hungry and probably getting restless. He focused His eyes on the One who's enough. He turned His face toward His Father, the God of abundance who's more than enough.

Then, in verse 16, Jesus "said a blessing." Jesus is the Son of God. So, the five loaves and two fish, the blessing from God that they were all about to eat, was also provided by Jesus. But then why did He feel the need to thank God for it by saying a blessing? I think that He did it to set an example for us of how we should behave. The five loaves and two fish weren't enough to feed the crowd. But Jesus thanked God for the "not enough" anyway. He thanked God for the food *before* there was enough, *then* the miracle happened. Gratitude precedes abundance.

Another lesson we see in this passage is that the disciples took the five loaves and two fish and gave them to Jesus. They surrendered what little was in their hands to have Jesus bless it. So, He took what they gave Him and broke it (verse 19). What happens when we give God all that we have and surrender ourselves fully to Him, only for it to seem like He takes everything and breaks it into pieces? When we ask Him to bless our family, our jobs, or even our pregnancies, but He hands it back to us broken? We surrender our lives to Him, and then things get messy. From our perspective, these things look damaged, worse off, tattered, and broken. But they're not just broken; they're also blessed. And the breaking had to happen before the blessing. When we hand Him what little we have and trust not only the blessing but also the breaking, God will multiply what we give Him. He makes it good and enough.

When Jesus gave back the bread to the disciples, it didn't magically multiply in that moment. The Bible never says, "Jesus blessed and broke the bread, then *poof*—there was an excess, and the disciples gave it to the people." No, when the disciples received the food from Jesus, it was the same amount of bread as before. So, when Jesus handed the bread and fish back to the disciples to distribute to the people, not only was it broken, but it was also still in the same form as before. There was the exact same amount.

Sometimes I expect to give my struggles or issues over to Jesus for Him to simply change them. That's not what He does here. He blessed the food and gave it to the disciples, and they moved their feet to be obedient and do what He had told them to do. *That's* when it multiplied—after their obedience. Jesus told the disciples in Matthew 14:16 to give the crowd something to eat. After Jesus blessed the food, broke it, and gave it back in the same amount, the disciples moved their feet. That was the show of obedience. That's what activated the miracle.

The disciples were obedient with the little they had. They didn't complain when Jesus handed the bread back to them in the same amount as before, according to all four accounts told in the Bible. They trusted the creator of the bread and the fish, their Savior, their Father, their Provider, and their friend. They had faith and obeyed. When they were obedient, that's when the state of what they were holding onto began to change and transform into what they hoped it would be.

FROM LACK TO OVERFLOW

Now, let's dive a little deeper into how this story ties into your miscarriage journey. At the very beginning of that passage of scripture, the people were waiting along the shore. Matthew 14:14 (ESV) says, "When [Jesus] went ashore he saw a great crowd, and he had compassion on them and healed their sick." The people were there to have Jesus heal them, and He did. He performed the miracles they asked Him to. But as the day came to a close, He knew they would be hungry soon. So, He instructed the disciples to give them something to eat. That means that Jesus prepared a way for the crowd on the shore to be fed, a blessing they didn't even know to ask Him for.

The people were there to be healed. They wanted physical healing, but Jesus knew they needed to be fed. Likewise, Jesus knows we want physical healing, but He wants to feed us spiritually.

Jesus meets the needs that we don't even know we have. He's a close God who understands our needs. He provides us with things we don't even know we need and things we don't even ask Him for in order to display His own glory.

What I asked Him for was a baby. What He gave me in that moment was more of Himself. He gave me a closer relationship with Him, a stronger bond between my husband and me, compassion and understanding for this issue of miscarriage and how common it is, friendships I didn't even know I needed, and a voice so I could be a source of encouragement for others going through this terrible heartache too.

About two weeks after my physical miscarriage, God very clearly laid it on my heart to start an online Bible study for women who had gone through miscarriages. About two months after that, He told me to write this book. I immediately considered myself unworthy for those types of platforms. I counted myself out. I told myself I wasn't a good enough speaker, a good enough writer. The enemy tried to tell me that I didn't have enough to say. *Who would want to hear what I have to say anyway?* I convinced myself. I was so terrified of failing and felt so inadequate. Even now, I still have those moments. Even as I'm writing this book, I often wonder, *Am I really going to be able to make a difference or help anyone with what I have to say?*

My voice, the Bible study, this book—they're my five loaves and two fish. They're not what I came to Jesus for. I wanted physical healing, a miracle, a different diagnosis, a baby, a family, a body that did what it was supposed to do. But instead, God wanted to feed me by giving me what He knew I needed more than all of those things. He wanted to give me this story to help other women make it through the pain I had been through to give my pain a purpose. He's using the things I didn't know to pray for as a way to invade my life and show off His own glory.

As He gave me my loaves and fish, though, just like in the story from the Bible, it didn't seem like enough. Inadequacies and doubts crowded my mind until my lack—of talent, worth, ability—became all I could see. But like the disciples, I decided to surrender my "not enough" to Him. He gave it back to me in the same form I handed it to Him. My talent and abilities were still the same as before: I don't have a special skill or creative writing degree now just because I surrendered this over to Him. I had never led a Bible study before and didn't magically know how to do it after I surrendered it to Him. No, from my own perspective, everything looked exactly the same. But this time, just like the actual loaves and fish, these things were now blessed.

I asked God for faith to take steps in obedience like the disciples did. It was hard. Moving headlong into something that, from my limited human perspective, looked like destruction and a setup for failure was terrifying. It's not easy to surrender, and it sure as heck isn't easy to take the "not enough" and be thankful. And now we're supposed to do both of those things *and* move our feet when our situation still doesn't look ideal? This wasn't what I signed up for. But again, I decided to trust the Lord because I knew He was worthy of my trust. He had never failed me before, and I knew He wouldn't start now. So, as I began to nervously move my feet, as I created the temporary Facebook group where we held a short six-week Bible study, as I shared my dream and vision of writing a book with my husband, that's when the miracle started to happen. That's when my loaves and fish became enough.

By encouraging other women to heal through that Bible study, I was also able to heal. So many of us even celebrated welcoming rainbow babies into the world. They were the babies we had prayed over together on Zoom. The miracles kept happening, just like in the story of the five loaves and two fish. That's when I was "coincidentally" connected to a book coach by a mutual friend (a friend who didn't even know I was planning to write a book!). Everything just began falling into place.

Please know that you don't have to wait to be fearless to move. I wasn't fearless by any means. That's not what God asks of me—or you. Jesus just told the disciples to go. He told me to start (the book, the Bible study). You can start moving *even though* you're still scared. *Even though* the road ahead is unknown and you're unsure of how it will all turn out.

A lot of my fears began to dissipate as I began moving my feet. I really think I would still be battling those fears if I hadn't taken steps toward obedience to what God had called me to do. It wasn't that I was confident in myself. No, it was my confidence in the Lord and the assurance that He was going to help me accomplish what He was calling me to do that prompted my movement.

As the disciples fed the people in the crowd, they had to keep reaching into the baskets, trusting that there would be enough. They kept reaching, in faith, as they passed each hungry person. They kept reaching for the provision. When we go through a similar season, where we feel like we have so little and need a miracle so that our "little" will be enough, we have to have the faith to keep reaching too. Not only do we have to keep reaching for the provision, but more importantly, we must keep reaching for the Provider. If we trust in faith and continue seeking God, we'll never run out.

In Matthew 14:20 (ESV), we find out what happened when the disciples continued to move in obedience. It says, "And they all ate and were satisfied. And they took up twelve baskets full of the broken pieces left over." We don't serve a God of lack. He's not a God of "just enough." He's not a God of either/or. We serve a God of abundance who takes not enough and turns it into overflow. The Bible tells us there were five thousand men in the crowd that were fed. Some scholars estimate that if we included the women and children in the count, the total would be closer to fifteen thousand people. Jesus took five loaves and two fish, which wasn't even enough for the disciples and Himself, and fed fifteen thousand people *and* had twelve basketfuls left over.

In John's account of the same story, he adds an extra part at the end: "When they had all had enough to eat, He said to His disciples, 'Gather the pieces that are left over. Let nothing be wasted'" (John 6:12 NIV). God doesn't waste our broken pieces. He uses everything broken, incomplete, or whole in our lives. These broken pieces are made significant in His hands. He's a God of details. Nothing escapes His notice; everything matters to Him.

God refusing to waste any broken pieces echoes the promise made in Romans 8:28 (NIV), "And we know that in all things God works for the good of those who love him, who have been called according to his purpose." He'll use our grief, pain, sorrow, mourning, weeping, and loss. This proves that there's purpose in our pain. It's not wasted.

Maybe you're starting to see that God has already begun giving you things that you didn't even know to ask for. Are there broken pieces you still need to surrender to Him? Is there worry you need to let go of? Is there fear you need to release? Whatever season you're in, whatever feelings of lack you have, He doesn't waste anything. He uses every piece for your good for His glory. These moments are the setup for a miracle. They're the preparation for a promise.

CHAPTER NINE

DEAR DIARY AND FORBIDDEN FRUIT

"Come to me, all you who are weary and burdened,
and I will give you rest . . . for I am gentle and humble in heart, and you will find rest for your souls."
—Matthew 11:28–29

I THINK WE CAN ALL AGREE THAT NO ONE LIKES THE DESERT SEA-son—especially when you're in the midst of it. But as we prog-ress through our journey, we'll slowly begin to understand why it had to happen. We begin to see the person we're transforming into during that season. We start to see the character He's shaped in us that's now able to sustain the blessing God has entrusted us with. Not only that, but as we move out of the desert season (yes, take heart, the desert season doesn't last forever!), we'll also see glimmers of redemption woven into our testimony as we enter into the promise.

I'm going to share with you an unfiltered excerpt straight from my journal on February 6, 2021, almost exactly four months after my miscarriage. To give you a reference point, at this point, we had been trying for a few months to conceive again, and I still wasn't pregnant. I had already started and completed the Bible study that God laid on my heart to do, and I had even started this very book He had asked me to write about my testimony and healing. But even though I was obedient, I still wasn't seeing the blessing.

As someone who has also suffered loss, my hope in sharing this with you is that you'll feel encouraged that you're not alone in your feelings. Even more so, though, my hope is that you will be comforted by the Lord and His response to me in that moment. That He'll give you a peace that "surpasses all understanding" through this reminder He gave me of His love and how He had redeemed my life through His Son, Jesus.

February 6, 2021
It's so hard not to look around at all that is lost. I have no bump. No pregnancy announcement. No pics. No nursery. No gender reveal. No sonograms. And my heart is so broken. It's so easy to get on Facebook and find someone who gave birth or who is announcing they're pregnant, and I'm struggling to see the good in all this. I've done everything right. I've done everything I've been asked, and I still don't have the blessing. I know that sounds selfish or arrogant, but God, Your word says obedience brings blessing (Deuteronomy 30). Where is the blessing? I want a baby so badly, and it seems like the one thing I don't have.

Then I waited for the Lord to speak to my heart, and here's what I heard Him say back to my spirit:

My greatest loss (giving up my one and only Son—John 3:16) was humanity's greatest gain. Not all that is lost is bad. I use everything for a purpose. This doesn't make sense on earth, but My ways and thoughts are higher (Isaiah 55:9). Though you operate in a world confined by space and time, trust Me moment by moment. I see the full picture. I see the past, the present, and eternity all at once, and if you could see that too, you'd fully understand what I'm doing.

But I'm too wise to allow you to see the picture as a whole because you'd try to walk ahead of me, without me, or you'd crumble under the weight of the "how" of it all. So, for now, I'm calling you to have faith. I'm working on things down on the inside of you that you have no idea about. And this lack of information isn't a desire for me to be illusive, but it's wisdom in giving you just what you need for today so that you seek me again tomorrow (Proverbs 25:1). Just like I did when I gave the Israelites manna (Exodus 16:1–36). If I had sent them into the Promise Land immediately, they would have missed the fundamental principles I taught them in the desert. And if I told them what was coming over the next 40 years of wandering in the wilderness, they would've trusted in their own strength or opted out altogether out of fear. Then they would've missed out on My greatest teachings and blessings in their life.

Your greatest desire is a baby whom you want to love and take care of. I was willing to give up (sacrifice) my one and only Son for the sake of humanity and their eternal blessing . . . Are you? Are you willing to sacrifice your own desires if that's what I require for your life? If you didn't have a baby and just

*had more of Me, would that be enough? What if your bless-
ings come in more than one form? What if your obedience not
only produces a baby but also produces fruit in the kingdom
and everlasting life for others you're reaching through your
pain? You've asked Me to help you understand the gravity of
my love for you. You're so in love with the idea of a baby that
doesn't exist yet. How much more do you comprehend my love
for you now? I was willing to send My only Son—whom I
also love—to die for you. Do you see it now? All of this has
always been FOR you.*

God reminded me of His character and the unwavering God
He's always been to me since the beginning of time, before the foun-
dations of the earth. He reminded me that He's worthy of my trust
and surrender. He gave up and surrendered His Son for me because
He loves me so much. As someone who has prayed daily for a baby,
I can't imagine having a child and then choosing to give them up for
the sake of humanity like God did. But He did. For me and for you.
Ephesians 3:18 (NIV) says, "[That you] may have power, together
with all the Lord's holy people, to grasp how wide and long and high
and deep is the love of Christ." His response to me in that moment
was a gentle call for me to surrender to that love. He asked me to
surrender to Him and trust Him, moment by moment.

GIVING UP CONTROL

Merriam-Webster defines "surrender" as "to yield to the power,
control, or possession of" (Merriam-Webster). Yielding up power
and control . . . Why is that so hard? I'm a big fan of control over
here. I love to feel like I have the power, even when I don't. I have

a tendency to manipulate situations in my favor in order to control them. When I had my miscarriage, I wanted to control the outcome. I think we all do. We want to change the situation so it will be what we desire, which is a healthy pregnancy. We want that baby back. We want a redo in the ultrasound room. We want to never go to the restroom again and see what we saw. We want to rewind time and do something differently to see if we get a new outcome. Even after I accepted that I had lost my baby, I wanted so badly to control the timeline of when I got pregnant again. I had been so ready to be a mom. And after finding out I was going to be a mom and then having that ripped from my grasp, I only desired it even more. I wanted to control the next pregnancy because, at times, I felt that I could do it better than God did it the first time. I thought that if I had control, if it was up to me, things would be better than they were.

This is why it's so important to pair surrender with those big, bold prayers. When we surrender, we surrender to God's authority to answer those bold prayers in whatever way He sees fit. The resistance to surrender goes all the way back to Adam and Eve in Genesis. God warned Adam and Eve not to eat the fruit from a certain tree in the garden, "the tree of the knowledge of good and evil" (Gen. 2:17 NIV). Adam and Eve did their best to obey God. Until the serpent arrived and . . . you know the story. It's from Genesis 3:1–7 (NIV):

> *Now the serpent was more crafty than any of the wild animals the Lord God had made. He said to the woman, "Did God really say, 'You must not eat from any tree in the garden'?" The woman said to the serpent, "We may eat fruit from the*

trees in the garden, but God did say, 'You must not eat fruit from the tree that is in the middle of the garden, and you must not touch it, or you will die.'" "You will not certainly die," the serpent said to the woman. "For God knows that when you eat from it your eyes will be opened, and you will be like God, knowing good and evil." When the woman saw that the fruit of the tree was good for food and pleasing to the eye, and also desirable for gaining wisdom, she took some and ate it. She also gave some to her husband, who was with her, and he ate it. Then the eyes of both of them were opened, and they realized they were naked; so they sewed fig leaves together and made coverings for themselves.

When Satan appeared to Adam and Eve in the form of a serpent, his temptation to them wasn't the fruit itself. He was tempting Adam and Eve to surrender to something *other* than God. They were tempted to surrender to a created thing. They desired wisdom more than God. They idolized the wisdom they'd receive from the tree over the One who *is* wisdom and who can provide infinite wisdom (1 Kings 3 NIV).

My refusal to surrender is fear that God isn't better than everything He's telling me to give Him. Have you ever wanted knowledge more than you wanted God? Have you ever wished that you could see where your story was going instead of turning to the One who's writing it? I can empathize with Adam and Eve because I know what it's like to resist surrender, even when God has been faithful to you.

Adam and Eve had full ownership and reign over the garden. The *only* thing that God said was off-limits was that one tree. They had abundance, lacked nothing, and were given dominion within this perfect garden. So, when the enemy came to tempt Adam and Eve, what's the first thing he pointed out? The one tree, the *only* tree in the entire garden that was off-limits to them. Satan does the same to us. He points out the lack in our lives and begs the question, "Is God really good? If He's really good, why does He withhold this *one* thing from you?"

What's the one thing you feel God is "keeping" from you? What feels off-limits or just out of reach? Maybe it's pregnancy, a baby, the family you always imagined. For Adam and Eve, God wanted to be the *source* of wisdom and contentment. In the same way, God wants to be *your* true source of contentment.

We were never meant to find satisfaction in a baby or a perfect family. But of course, that doesn't mean that we can't want those things or even that we shouldn't. God just wants our hearts, and He wants us to seek Him for those gifts, not a created thing. Satan isn't clever, and he doesn't have any new tricks. He uses the same tactics on us that he used on Adam and Eve in the garden. His goal is to get us to focus on what's "empty," what seems out of reach or off-limits.

A lack of surrender is the false belief that when my hands are empty, God isn't big enough to fill them up again. On the other hand, when we do surrender, it's because we understand that there's nothing in our hands that God won't replace with more of Himself.

ANYTHING FOR EVERYTHING

There's a powerful story of surrender found in the Bible about a woman named Hannah, one of Elkanah's two wives, who asked God for a son: "Whenever the day came for Elkanah to sacrifice, he would give portions of the meat to his wife Peninnah and to all her sons and daughters. But to Hannah he gave a double portion because he loved her, and the Lord had closed her womb. Because the Lord had closed Hannah's womb, her rival kept provoking her in order to irritate her" (1 Sam. 1:4–6 NIV)

If we pause the story there and skip down to verses 10 and 11, we see Hannah's prayer for a son: "In her deep anguish Hannah prayed to the Lord, weeping bitterly. And she made a vow, saying, 'Lord Almighty, if you will only look on your servant's misery and remember me, and not forget your servant but give her a son, then I will give him to the Lord for all the days of his life, and no razor will ever be used on his head.'"

The thing Hannah wanted more than anything else in the entire world was a son. But when she presented her request to God, she offered him back to God in the same breath. How could she ask for something she so desperately wanted and yet, in the same sentence, surrender her unborn son back to God? The answer to that question is found a few verses later in 1 Samuel 2:1 (NIV): "Then Hannah prayed and said: 'My heart rejoices in the Lord; in the Lord my horn is lifted high. My mouth boasts over my enemies, for I delight in your deliverance.'" She exalted herself in the Lord. She delighted in who God is. She was willing to surrender *anything* because she believed God was *everything*.

Blessings come (in many different forms) *after* we surrender. 1 Samuel 1:20 (NIV) says, "So in the course of time Hannah became pregnant and gave birth to a son. She named him Samuel, saying, 'Because I asked the Lord for him.'"

Let me clarify, though. I don't want you to think that if you surrender, everything will go according to plan. And I definitely don't want you to surrender just in the hopes of receiving a blessing. Surrendering doesn't mean you always get what you want, and surrender certainly doesn't equal "simple." But your acts of obedience and surrender open up the doors to allow blessings to flow to you and through you.

It's easier to surrender when we know who it is we're surrendering to—when we understand the character of God. We're surrendering to a God who loves us more than we love ourselves. He knows us better than we know ourselves. He's a good God who sees through the depths of things we can't. This was extremely hard for me to put into practice during my miscarriage, though. I had to surrender the very thing I wanted most—having a baby. The Lord had to get my attention a few different ways before I would finally understand the importance of complete surrender.

What do you need to surrender to the Lord? Is there anything you're holding onto out of fear that God won't, or can't, come through for you? How can you practice surrender, even in the small things? We can find peace in surrendering *anything* once we put our full trust in the One who's *everything*.

CHAPTER TEN

GOLDEN RETRIEVERS AND

FIRE WALKERS

"'For my thoughts are not your thoughts, neither are your ways my ways,' declares the Lord. 'As the heavens are higher than the earth, so are my ways higher than your ways and my thoughts than your thoughts.'"
—Isaiah 55:8–9

I SAIAH 55:8–9 HAS ALWAYS BEEN ONE OF THOSE STICK-IT-ON-A-poster, hang-it-up-in-church kind of verses for me. You know the ones? The verses that sound really good, the ones many of us heard growing up in church. It wasn't until I went through my miscarriage that I really tried to digest this verse and what it actually meant. I've always known that God knows best, but what did that mean for me in *this* season? How could *this* possibly be God's best when it felt like my worst? How could this possibly be better for me than having a happy, healthy child? How could His ways possibly make more sense than mine?

A few weeks after my miscarriage, I had a day where the emotional pain became so intense and hurt welled up so deep inside of my bones that I just began spilling my guts to God and asking Him all of the *why* questions: Why me? Why now? Why do *they* get to have this blessing, and I don't?

I know I can't be the only one who asked those kinds of questions after a miscarriage. Maybe you've been asking the same ones. And you should. There's so much freedom to be found in pouring our hearts out to God and telling Him all the things we're thinking but feel we are too "holy" to say out loud.

It was in that moment that He used my five-year-old golden retriever, Nala, to help me understand what Isaiah 55:8–9 truly meant.

When she was a puppy, Nala had several stomach conditions that led to her needing to be on a bland diet of chicken and white rice for a while. One day, while I was cooking her meal, Nala walked into the kitchen. She smelled the aroma of something she desired. She sat beneath my feet next to the stove and made eye contact. If you have a dog, you know what that means. She licked her lips as if to say, "Mom, please?" Her stomach had been unsettled for days, and she hadn't been able to keep anything down. She was hungry. And the food was right there. I had every capability in that moment to give her what she desired—the food. But it wasn't quite ready.

I grabbed a spatula and moved the cooked chicken from the pan onto a cutting board so I could chop it into smaller pieces that were easier for her to consume. Once it was chopped up, I picked up her food bowl from the floor and placed it on the counter. Then I dumped the chopped chicken into it. I scooped some white rice over the top of the chicken. Nala's begging intensified. She was now wagging her tail, drooling, licking her lips, and doing the excited dance she does, her two front paws bouncing back and forth. The bowl remained on the counter, and I told her she had to wait.

She started whimpering. She wanted the food when she smelled it. And she knew her food bowl. So, when I placed the food in her dog bowl, she knew it belonged to her. So why wasn't I giving it to her? Was I playing games with her? Was I being cruel? She was hungry. I had the ability to feed her, but in that moment, I chose not to. If she were human, she would've asked me *why?* Why withhold something from me if you have the ability to just bless me with it?

It was because I knew something she didn't know. I knew that the chicken and rice were scorching hot. If given to her in that moment, it would've burned her mouth. Instead of it being good for her, it would've hurt her tongue and caused more pain. Giving her that food right away would've done more harm than good, even if she couldn't understand that.

This serves as an example of how even good, holy, perfect things that are meant to be a blessing can be detrimental if given at the wrong time. Nala didn't have to tell me what she needed. She didn't even have the capacity to know that chicken and rice would settle her stomach. She couldn't see the bigger picture that I could and didn't have the resources to research it like I did. She felt the pain, and I had the solution. I began cooking it before she was starving in preparation for her hunger.

Just like I stood over the stove preparing food for Nala, the Lord prepares our blessings for us. He's detailed in His preparation. Just like I knew exactly how and when to prepare Nala's food, God designs our blessing specifically for us, with us in mind to receive it. I did the research. I cooked the meal. I scooped it into her bowl. And at the right time, I gave it to her. Nala's only role in this transaction was to patiently trust and gladly receive. So it is with us. God's thoughts are higher than ours, and we have to trust that He is for us, not against us (Rom. 8:31 NIV). We know that

He works all things together for the good of those who love Him and are called according to His purpose (Rom. 8:28 NIV), that His ways are higher (Isa. 55:8–9 NIV), and that He sees the bigger picture of what's going on that we can't begin to grasp. Yet, even so, His ways and timing aren't ours. But His plan and purpose are good. Jeremiah 29:11 (NIV) says, "'For I know the plans I have for you,' declares the Lord, 'plans to prosper you and not to harm you, plans to give you hope and a future.'"

I know it's hard to trust God when we sometimes perceive that we'd do a better job handling our own situation. But there's a reason behind what He's doing, even if we can't comprehend it. Sometimes, we see His making us wait as a sign that He doesn't care. We think that maybe the Lord is withholding something good from us or that He's being harsh. But what I had to learn is that there's purpose in the waiting: it's so that our blessing will be for our highest good.

That day, when it was finally dinner time and the food had cooled inside Nala's silver dog bowl, I set it on the ground. She devoured it. By the time I gave her the food, she had become hungry enough to enjoy it. She had waited in anticipation, with patience. And during the wait, her desire for the food had grown, so she was even more thankful when she received it. After a few days of this bland diet and some antibiotics, Nala was back to her normal self.

When we are waiting on God, we have to learn to surrender to His timing and His ways. In the waiting period, it was so easy for me to become consumed with the things I wanted that I forgot how mighty God was. I didn't stop to consider what He wanted to show me in my waiting. So often, I try to manipulate the situations I'm in to gain control and force things to happen at the perfect time for me. But what I want you to know is that when you and I seek God more than we seek the blessing, the tectonic plates of our hearts begin to shift.

My desires started to change to reflect God's own desires for my life. The doors in my life I would've had to beat down to try and open on my own were gently opened before me by the Lord when I sought Him more than His blessing. When I surrendered to the Lord and His timing, He created divine appointments to get me exactly where He wanted me to be—even if that wasn't the place I saw myself.

When I look back on seasons and events in my life, including my miscarriage, I see the evidence of God's ways being higher than mine. I'm starting to see so many things in my life align that show me why I had to go through the hard stuff, and that has made it slightly more bearable. I'm starting to see the good in it that God promised to me. But you may not be there yet. In fact, we won't *always* see the purpose of our pain on this side of eternity. That's why we're called to have faith. But we're much more likely to notice the purpose of our pain when we're actively searching for God and His goodness.

You may feel like you're stuck, not moving forward, or even behind because of your loss. The truth is, you can trust that even though your life may seem stagnant right now, God's working behind the scenes, preparing. He's gently opening up doors that you could never break through on your own. The preparation for your promise is specific to you. It may not seem like the waiting has meaning in the moment. At times, the pursuit of patience may seem cruel, but you can trust that God's ways are higher and that He's a good, faithful, and trustworthy God—even if His ways don't make sense to you right now. So, hold tight to the hope that your "chicken and rice" are coming, in the right form and at the right time, from the loving Father, whose greatest desire has always been to give us those things.

However, *true* surrender isn't only surrendering to God's timing. It's also surrendering to God's plans.

EVEN IF YOU DON'T

It's one thing to relinquish *timing* when you go through a miscarriage. It's one thing to grasp the concept of how to surrender to His timing of our plans, to trust that He will do what we think is best *when* He thinks it's best. But it's a whole other ball game to surrender to God's timing *and* plans, especially when His plans may not match yours.

I would say things to God like, "Okay, I surrender my future to You, and I trust Your timing in making me a mother." I knew when I had my miscarriage that I would one day learn to live with the pain. I could cope with the devastation I was facing because I held out hope that one day soon, I would still be a mother. I saw a light at the end of the tunnel for myself. I held firm to the faith that my story would have a happy ending, one where I became a mom.

The key to us truly trusting the Lord, though, is to become so surrendered that we echo the words of Shadrach, Meshach, and Abednego from the Bible and say to God, "But even if You don't."

If you're not familiar with who the heck those three men are, let me explain. Their king, King Nebuchadnezzar, built a gold statue of himself and gathered all the people around to worship it. In fact, the king proclaimed that "Whoever does not fall down and worship shall immediately be cast into a burning fiery furnace" (Dan. 3:6 ESV).

Shadrach, Meshach, and Abednego refused to bow down to their king. They were Jews, and they served the one and only true God and knew that no one and nothing was worthy of their worship except Him. When King Nebuchadnezzar heard this news, he demanded in a furious rage that they be brought before him. When the three men stood before the king, he threatened to throw them into the blazing furnace if they didn't bow down and worship the statue. "And then what god will be able to rescue you from my power?" he asked them (Dan. 3:15 NLT).

"Shadrach, Meshach, and Abednego replied, 'O Nebuchadnezzar, we do not need to defend ourselves before you. If we are thrown into the blazing furnace, the God whom we serve is able to save us. He will rescue us from your power, Your Majesty. But even if he doesn't, we want to make it clear to you, Your Majesty, that we will never serve your gods or worship the gold statue you have set up'" (Dan. 3:16–18 NLT). The king was furious and threw Shadrach, Meshach, and Abednego into the fiery furnace. And that's where their miracle took place—in the flames. The king was amazed to look into the fire and see not three but four men walking around unharmed. He was shocked and confused and believed it to be an angel of their God. He demanded that Shadrach, Meshach, and Abednego come out of the flames, and they did— unharmed. Amazed, the king promoted them to a higher status in the kingdom than before and never forgot the miracle he witnessed.

Shadrach, Meshach, and Abednego were extremely bold and brave. They were committed to serving the Lord, and only Him, no matter what. They surrendered to the God they knew could save them from the fiery furnace. That day, King Nebuchadnezzar believed in God as a result.

How often are we thrown into our own fiery furnaces of life, knowing that God could spare us the pain of ever having to endure them in the first place? That's how I felt when I went through my miscarriage. It was my fiery furnace, and I knew that God had the power to save me from going through this pain at all. He could have stepped in and saved me before I was thrown into the fire, before I lost my baby. But He didn't. He often allows us to go through trials like these to display His glory through us. Just like with Shadrach, Meshach, and Abednego.

These three men went up to the king, knowing the consequences of not bowing down to him, but they still refused. They remained faithful to God. If I were them, I would've probably assumed in that moment that God was going to reward me for my faith by changing the king's mind so that I'd never actually have to be thrown into the fire. I mean, after all, I was risking my life enough just by choosing to only worship the one true God and keep His commandments. So, surely God wouldn't allow me to be punished by the king or go through this literal fire. Surely God would rescue me before the fiery furnace. Surely God would see my faith and rescue me before I have to endure something as painful as a miscarriage.

But the men were thrown into the fire despite their faith in God and His ability to rescue them. Not only that, but the king heated the fire seven times hotter than usual, tied the three men up fully clothed, and threw them into the fire. Even the men who threw them in there died because of how hot the fire was—they burned just for standing near it. Before we start imagining this story as a fairy tale that didn't actually happen, we have to remember that it did.

The fire was real—just like the fires you face now. It was really hot, and this story truly did happen. And we have to put ourselves in the shoes (that should've been melted, by the way, but weren't) of these men and remember that they had no idea what was going to happen to them. This story gets watered down as we hear it more and more often, to the point that we miss the gravity and reality of how terrifying that situation would've been for these three men. It's vital that we remember these were real men with real skin and feelings and family, just like you and I have. But they believed God was worth everything they risked losing.

Not only did they live, but the Bible says, "The fire had not touched them. Not a hair on their heads was singed, and their clothing was not scorched. They didn't even smell of smoke!" (Dan. 3:27 NLT). After the fire, we learn why it had to happen. Immediately after seeing the men still alive and completely untouched by the fire, King Nebuchadnezzar said, "Praise to the God of Shadrach, Meshach, and Abednego! . . . Therefore, I make this decree: If any people, whatever their race or nation or language, speak a word against the God of Shadrach, Meshach, and Abednego, they will be torn limb from limb, and their houses will be turned into heaps of rubble. There is no other god who can rescue like this!" (Dan. 3:28–29 NLT).

These men didn't have to endure this fiery furnace just for themselves. Of course, the Lord used it to grow their faith, but we see another reason why the men needed to go through this. It was partially because King Nebuchadnezzar gave His life over to God that day and chose Him and the one and only true Lord as a result of watching them go through this fire unharmed.

Sometimes, God will call us to walk through the unknown. He'll test our faith (James 1:3 NIV) and allow us to go through fires. Not only will we not die, but we'll also come out the other side unharmed, untouched by the fiery pain we think is going to consume us, even when the fires are heated up seven times hotter for us and we have to go through things we don't think we'll make it out of alive. That's how I often felt while walking through my miscarriage journey. It felt like I was going to be in the fire forever, just getting burned over and over. It was lonely, and I couldn't see the light at the other end of the tunnel.

Distraught, angry, bitter, closed off, shut down, depressed, anxious, worthless, hopeless—these are some of the emotions you may expect to have after a miscarriage. It would even be understandable if you felt all of those things—I know I did for a season. But that's not how my story ended. That's how I looked in the fire, but the fire didn't consume me. It didn't take me out. It won't scientifically make sense to us or others how we go through something like a miscarriage and come out with stronger faith and a sense of peace that surpasses understanding when we should be emotionally dead. This is why the Bible says, "Count it all joy, my brothers, when you meet trials of various kinds, for you know that the testing of your faith produces steadfastness. And let steadfastness have its full effect, that you may be perfect and complete, lacking in nothing" (James 1:2–4 ESV).

Our fiery furnaces weren't meant to harm us. The fire grows our own faith. But our fires are also a testimony to others. When the people around us see our faith and how we surrender to the

Lord and His timing and His plans, they may begin seeking the God that we serve, just like King Nebuchadnezzar did. And what a privilege it was for these men to be the ones who led the king of their land to the Lord! All because they were willing, surrendered vessels to the Lord's plans and had their eyes focused on worshipping Him alone.

They didn't just surrender to God because they knew He could save them. They were also so surrendered to Him that they were prepared to follow through in obedience, whatever their fate was—even if God decided not to save them. I'm sure their ideal plan was to *not* go into the fire at all and for the king to have a change of heart. That would've been my ideal scenario, for sure. But Shadrach, Meshach, and Abednego weren't just surrendered to the timing of God. They were also fully surrendered to His plan and His will, even if it would cost them their very lives.

This is the hardest part, isn't it? I realized that even after surrendering to God's timing, I wasn't finished. I still had to surrender to the Lord's plan for my future. I had to surrender to His plan for me and my husband and our family. Even though I didn't know why He allowed this miscarriage to happen, I knew He'd make it good.

I had my own idea of what would make this story or season good. It would be getting pregnant again right afterward and being a mom someday. That was my version of what it would look like for God to rescue me from my fiery furnace. But I had to surrender my hopes to Him too. I had to release the idea that I had control over whether or not my happily ever after would end in me being a mama someday. I realized that me having a baby right away might not be part of God's plan. I had to make the hard choice daily to surrender to His timing for me to become a mother. But that was only the first layer.

I felt the Lord calling me deeper to surrender to His plans "even if He doesn't," even if the end of my story doesn't look the way I pictured it to or the way I thought it should. Would I surrender the outcome even if it wasn't what I desired? What if His plans for my life didn't include me ever giving birth to my own biological child? Would I still surrender not only to God's timing but also to His choices? Will you?

Sometimes God doesn't remove us from the fire; He just meets us in it. He does this so we can testify that there were seasons in our lives where everyone, including us, thought we'd be consumed by the trials surrounding us, but God's presence covered us so heavily that we can go through experiences that feel like fire and come out the other side without even the smell of smoke on us. That's my hope and prayer for you—that you'll make the daily choice to surrender your life to God's timing *and* His plans, knowing that His ways and thoughts are higher than your own.

YOU OWN THE YES

My surrender to God's plans wasn't a single moment in time. It wasn't one decision I made once. It was an intentional decision at every moment to continually surrender every minute of every day. I realized that God owns everything, and I just own my yes—my yes to His timing, His plans, and the things He allows or withholds.

Before I started writing this book, the Lord laid it on my heart to take a sabbatical. I work in social media, so His challenge to me was to fast from social media for that week, which meant I couldn't work. As the breadwinner of our family, that terrified me.

But the thought kept popping up until I couldn't ignore it anymore. So, I took that sabbatical for a week in obedient surrender.

When I did, I wanted God to give me clarity and answers about so many things I had been praying about in my life. I wanted Him to show me what direction He wanted me to take in my life. For the first three days, I asked the Lord to show me where He wanted me to go and what He wanted me to do. I asked for Him to speak to me and to give me those answers as I studied His Word. And on the third day, I heard the still small voice of the Lord that said, "What if the blessing for your obedience to take this sabbatical isn't answers? What if the prize of your sabbatical this week is just more of Me? Will that be enough for you?"

Ouch. I decided to change my prayers from asking Him for the things I *wanted* to asking Him to show me more of Himself. And on the fourth day of my sabbatical, I finally started gaining clarity on what He wanted me to do in that season of my life. He was gracious enough to reveal those things to me, but it wasn't until I started seeking *Him* more than I was seeking the plan itself. That's when He began to show me glimpses of the redemption He would have in the story I was about to begin writing.

I'm writing this book a full year after God laid it on my heart to do so. But I'm being faithful to His calling. He's woven together so many beautiful pieces of my story already, simply because I begged for more of Him and surrendered to His timing and, ultimately, His plan for me. It took a lot of work to get here, but I can honestly say that I am now totally surrendered to what He wants to do in and through me. It was a hard road to walk to get here, but seeing His provisions and His faithfulness, I'm reminded that He's worthy of my surrender.

What are some things you still need to surrender to God so that He can begin to use your story too? What little glimmers of redemption can you already see in your story as you look back on where you've been and how far you've come?

CHAPTER ELEVEN

SUDDEN SURGERIES AND

SECOND TRIES

"And after you have suffered a little while, the God of
all grace, who has called you to His eternal glory in
Christ, will Himself restore, confirm, strengthen, and
establish you." —1 Peter 5:10

AFTER ALL THE CHAOS OF OUR ULTRASOUND AND THE UNRE-
solved questions we had leaving the doctor's office, my husband and I made the heartbreaking choice to let my body natu-
rally miscarry. Because of the nature of the type of miscarriage I
had, there wasn't enough evidence for me in my situation to feel
comfortable taking anything at home or going to the doctor for a
procedure to end the pregnancy. I know some of my hesitation was
because I was in denial because I so desperately wanted to change
my diagnosis. I thought that if I just waited it out, then something
miraculous would happen. It didn't.

We first heard the news of our miscarriage at our ultrasound
on October 28. After that, it was a slow, gradual process of loss,
which made it sting that much more. The anguish of losing our
baby was bad enough without it dragging on. My body didn't even
show signs of miscarriage until November 7. Even after that, it was
still an entire week before I fully miscarried.

If you've gone through this experience yourself, it may be hard to relive those moments. I understand. But I'm going to share the day of my miscarriage with you in the hopes that it makes you feel a little less alone, a little more seen. It was one of the hardest days of my life, and it's a miracle that I made it through. But I did, and so did you.

The weekend after I began spotting in the truck bed, we celebrated my father-in-law's birthday at their cozy home about an hour away. We spent the day with our family. We grilled and played games in the backyard, bundled up in winter coats. Despite the fun, I felt very "off" that entire day. I told my mother- and sister-in-law, both of whom have children, that my stomach felt very hard. I asked them to feel it, and they both said I was having contractions, or Braxton Hicks. It was strange to hear that.

Normally, contractions are a sign of impending labor, and women get excited about them. Normally, these sensations are followed by little baby cries, learning the ropes of being a mom (or being a mom again), and all the excitement of family and friends who can't wait to meet the newest addition.

It was strange because I knew that my hopes for each of those things were about to come crashing down when we finally lost the baby. I just wanted the state of limbo, the waiting, and the unknown to all be over so we could move forward and truly begin to heal. But it was like I didn't want to put the effort into healing before we actually lost the baby. I knew that it would hurt that much more when it finally happened and that all those wounds I had worked so hard to heal were going to be ripped back open.

So, when I heard I was having contractions, I felt a flood of opposing feelings rushing through my brain: hopeful that the end of this chapter was nearing; crushed that this chapter had to end this way; sad that I was experiencing these odd feelings and this pain for the first time and couldn't even be excited about it because I knew what normally followed all of those sensations wasn't going to happen for me; concerned for the unknown that was going to be both emotionally and physically painful as I endured the impending loss of the baby; disappointed that I was going to go through all the physical pain for nothing—no baby, no bows, no swaddles, no middle-of-the-night wake-ups. No, when they said I was having contractions that day, I knew that it was the beginning of the end, an end I never would've chosen for myself.

Although I didn't feel well, I powered through so we could enjoy the birthday celebrations. On our drive home that night, I talked to my dad on the phone while my husband was driving. I just remember having shooting pains all through my abdomen and having to mute the phone to breathe through them. I didn't mention it to my dad. It was painful and something I had never felt before. We made it home, and that night and the next day were like any other day I'd had in the last two weeks—gloomy, lonesome, and difficult.

Sunday, November 15, 2020—after over two weeks of a diagnosed miscarriage and nothing but spotting, Braxton Hicks, and sharp, shooting pains to prove that anything might have been wrong—I was still technically "pregnant." That night, I made dinner for Derek and myself. I can still remember the exact meal—BBQ chicken, macaroni and cheese, and great northern beans. It was one of my favorite meals growing up, and I had a random craving for it. Little did I know that I'd never get a chance to eat it.

As I was cooking the food, I kept pausing. I would drop down on my knees, wince in pain, and get right back up and continue cooking. As my husband watched, he said, "Are you sure you're okay? Do you want me to cook? Why don't you go lay down? We can just order a pizza." But, stubborn as ever, I insisted on powering through. I thought it was just a bad stomachache, but when I went to the bathroom and saw the blood, I knew it was finally happening.

Miscarrying was something I never thought I would have to go through. So, when I found out it was an inevitable part of my story, I wanted a miracle. When I came to terms with the fact that I probably wasn't going to get my miracle in the way I had hoped, I just wanted the whole thing to be over and done with.

Then, when my body took 19 days to find out what my head already knew, that this pregnancy was no longer viable, every 24 hours was grueling. It felt like torture to not only have to live through something like that but also to live in the in-between for so long.

When I went to the bathroom, I saw what I had both dreaded (because it meant it was true) and prayed for (because it meant it was over) starting to happen. After dinner, Derek had gone to work for an hour, something he did every Sunday night to prepare for the week ahead. In the hour he was gone, things went from bad to worse. The pain intensified, and I called my mom, who's a nurse. It was as painful emotionally as it was physically.

When the pain became physically unbearable, I called my husband to come home and take me to the hospital because I knew something was wrong. He worked about ten minutes away, but that night it took him only six minutes to get home. When he got there, we grabbed the necessities and were at the hospital in record time. We arrived at the emergency room around 11 pm on Sunday, November 15.

I ran inside and put myself in a wheelchair next to the check-in desk. I ignored the questions of the woman behind the counter and begged someone to wheel me into a room and give me pain medication. My husband rushed in behind me to get me checked in as they wheeled me to a room. They gave me multiple doses of morphine because my body was in shock, and I was about to pass out from the pain. We ended up staying in the hospital all night long. My husband, who had to be at work at 5:30 am the next day, didn't leave my side for a second.

That night was painful in every way imaginable. I remember sitting in the hospital bed as the morphine began to kick in, telling my husband that I wished this pain was for something. I remember telling him that I would have been so happy to go through this pain if a baby was the gift I received at the end of it. But the worst part about the pain was knowing I would still be leaving the hospital empty-handed.

I asked him to text our family and update them. Then I asked him to turn on worship music. We listened to Kari Jobe, Christy Nockels, and Elevation Worship for hours. I lifted my hands, wrists covered in hospital bands and IV wires, tears streaming down my face, and morphine masking the pain. And I promised God in that moment that no matter what He allowed me to go through, I would continually praise Him. Because with faith, I knew that He was still good.

Even in the timing of me starting to lose the baby that night, I saw His goodness and faithfulness. We weren't at Derek's parents' house. We weren't driving down the road. Derek wasn't at work when he wasn't able to leave. God timed it so that I would have help quickly and so that I wouldn't have to be alone.

That night in the hospital, I lost a lot of blood, but I was starting to feel a little better after I had passed everything. When they readied to discharge me, the nurse came into the room, walked toward the left side of my bed, and stood next to Derek. She explained that she was going to sit me up first and have me stay in that position before having me stand up to move into the wheelchair. But as Derek and the nurse sat me up, I passed out. I fell off the side of the bed into my husband's arms.

Swarms of nurses and doctors rushed into the room. As I came to, I saw a bright light above me and tons of masks and eyes staring back at me. They determined that the reason for me passing out was because my blood pressure had dropped dangerously low and that I couldn't afford to lose any more blood. But I was still bleeding.

At around 5:30 am on Monday, November 16, the OB on call decided that a D&C, or a dilation and curettage procedure, would be the best treatment option to stop the bleeding. At 7 am, he performed the surgery. By 9:30 am, I was back home and finally going to sleep after the longest night of my life.

Less than two months before, on September 30, when I found out I was pregnant, never in my wildest dreams could I have imagined we'd end up here. *How did this happen? How did I get here? This kind of thing doesn't happen to people like me.* Until it did.

TRYING AGAIN

After a meeting with my OB and discussing the trauma my body had endured during the miscarriage, she was very straightforward about the amount of time my husband and I needed to wait to start trying again. She wanted me to wait to get my period back. Then, we could start trying for a baby again that next cycle. I was so ready to start trying again, and my husband said he was ready whenever I was.

I felt bad at the time for being so ready to be pregnant again. I worried that maybe I wasn't emotionally healing well. Maybe I was so ready to have another baby because I wanted to mask the pain I was feeling. I second-guessed myself and worried that I wasn't waiting long enough to grieve the loss of my first baby. I felt so guilty because I didn't want to seem like I was moving on from our first child too quickly or not honoring their life properly. I knew I loved that baby and that no baby could ever replace them or the gaping hole that they left in our hearts. I had wanted a baby so badly, and when we found out we were pregnant, I was so excited. So, I think it was natural for me to be even more ready for a baby after I had one in my grasp, and it was seemingly ripped right out from under me.

I knew the reason behind being ready so quickly was pure. I think it's important to take limits off the shoulds, coulds, and woulds of miscarriage. There's no right or wrong, no black-or-white way to grieve or cope. One woman might be ready right away to start trying again. Another may need a few years to be ready to try again. Some may be so scarred from the loss that they never want to try again. And I think it should all be okay. I don't think we need to fit the timeline of miscarriage into a box and become judgmental when other people heal differently or at different paces than we do.

We decided to listen to my OB because she knew what was best. She wanted to give my body the best chance at having a successful pregnancy the next time. So, we began trying again when we got the green light. Not to be graphic or go into too much detail, but when you're trying for a baby, it can seem like a job. Girl, you know what I'm talking about. Test strips, downloading 18 ovulation apps, watching the calendar, planning out your day to make time with your husband . . . the list goes on. It can feel daunting, like a chore.

If I can be honest with you (and I've already been honest with my husband), there were times when we were trying that I genuinely just wanted a baby more than I wanted intimacy with my husband. I absolutely love my husband, okay? And he's *hot*. I mean, on a scale of one to ten, he's a twelve kind of hot. It wasn't him or anything he was or wasn't doing. I'm embarrassed to admit it, but there were times I had sex with him in the past just because I wanted a baby so badly. At times, I lost sight of the present moment because I just wanted the future result.

How often do you take this transactional approach with God? Where you pray and spend time in His Word or go to church because of something you hope He'll give you? How often are you close with God because you're more interested in getting whatever you're praying for than in knowing Him more? It can be so easy to get so into the rhythm of what you're "expected" to do that you treat intimacy with God like a chore.

We check our calendars and mark it off our to-do lists. We water down what a blessing it is to have the ability to even draw near to God, and we begin to seek His gifts and blessings more than we desire God Himself. We want what He can give us more than we want Him.

I'll be the first to admit I'm guilty of this. When we begin to notice that in our lives, I hope we get back to the root of our relationship with Him and ask Him to help us to grow in our desire for Him, that we'll ask Him to help us to want to spend time with Him just to get to know Him more.

Derek and I tried for several months to get pregnant again. Those months in between the pain and the purpose—those were the toughest. It was such a trying time in my life. I didn't really know who I was. I had a major identity crisis. I was struggling to come to terms with the fact that I would've been four, five, six months along in my pregnancy, and here I was still trying to conceive. Almost daily, I had to battle the idea that I was behind.

GLIMMERS OF REDEMPTION

By spring of 2021, nothing felt different for me except for the fact that I would get out of breath just from tying my shoes. That's the one symptom I remember before I took the pregnancy test. On the morning of March 4, 2021, I woke up and immediately took a pregnancy test. I was ten days post-ovulation and had been counting down the days during that "two-week wait." I knew it would probably be too soon, but they say it's possible to get a positive around that time. So, I figured, why not?

During that grueling three-minute wait (that actually felt like years), I prepared myself for the heartbreak I knew I'd feel if there was only one stark, pink line. I stood on the other side of the bathroom as I waited for my timer to make its way down to zero. During those three minutes, I prayed and asked God to please bless me with this miracle—the same blessing I had prayed for every month before but didn't get. I sang a worship song out loud, more so to distract myself than an act of worship, if I'm being honest.

The timer went off. I slowly walked toward the pregnancy test that lay there on our black granite countertop. I had my eyes only halfway opened, butterflies in my stomach. Even though I was trying not to get my hopes up, I couldn't help it. As I stood over the test, I fully opened my eyes. My jaw dropped. I quickly cupped my right hand over my mouth. I snatched the test off the counter and opened my eyes wider. I couldn't believe what I saw. One stark, pink line and, to the left of it, the faintest pink line. It was faint, but it was there.

I turned on another light in the bathroom to get a better look. Sure enough, there were the two pink lines I had been praying for. I cried. Then I panicked. *What if it happens again? I don't think my heart can take another loss,* I thought.

I was about to take a shower and get ready for the day, so I turned on the song "Famous For" by Tauren Wells, the same guy who sings "Hills and Valleys." I knew the catchy chorus by heart. The song recounts pivotal times in the Bible where God showed up: when He parted the Red Sea; when He was in the fire with Shadrach, Meshach, and Abednego; when He saved Daniel in the lions' den by shutting the lions' mouths; and when He brought dry bones to life again, as told in the book of Ezekiel. The song then asks God to do what He's famous for—showing up and making good on His promises.

As the music blared through the speaker on my iPhone, I sang those words in the shower loudly. I spoke them to my soul, pleading with the Lord—on behalf of me, Derek, and this brand-new, teeny baby—to do what He was famous for. To let this pregnancy, this baby, be a testament to His redemption in my life. To prove what I knew all along—that there was purpose in my pain.

After my shower, I called my OB right away to let her know I was pregnant. She was excited but wanted to do some blood work to check my progesterone levels (which, thankfully, turned out to be normal). After getting off the phone with my OB, I found Derek in the hallway and shared the news. We had been trying for a long time and keeping track of my cycle, so he knew I was taking a test that day. When I shared the news, he was excited but scared. We both were.

Getting pregnant after you've had a loss should be the happiest day of your life. But if you've experienced that day, you also know it's one of the scariest. It was so hard for me to be excited and feel confident in my pregnancy after losing my first baby. At that point, I had never had a healthy pregnancy. I couldn't even fathom what that would be like. At that point, the only feelings I knew following a pregnancy test were loss and devastation. So, that's immediately what my mind ran to.

That whole morning, I was a ball of emotions.

I cried happy tears and thanked the Lord for this blessing, this miracle. In the same breath, I pleaded with the Lord to let this baby live and not to allow anything to happen this time. I was stressed to the max. I was so anxious and nervous.

A PRAYER FOR THE FEARFUL

If you're reading this from that place I was in—terrified and pregnant after loss or maybe scared to even try for another baby—I understand. I know the fear can be paralyzing. No matter where you are in your journey, here's what I want you to know: God's in control.

When I found out that I was pregnant again, I wanted to feel in control. I wanted to keep that baby safe. I lived in constant fear of what might happen. I couldn't bear the thought of having to go through another loss. There were times when I wanted my baby to hurry up and be born just so I could keep it safe.

Then the Lord reminded me of something. I realized that baby—my baby, your baby—was *God's* first. He loves them more than we do. I know; I can't comprehend it either. But He created them. He knows them by name and has called them for a purpose (Jeremiah 29:11 NIV), which He will carry out until completion (Phil. 1:6 NIV). The looser our grip on our children (unborn, passed, or born), the more we display our faith that the *Lord's* plans are best, not ours. I know; it's not easy. But this is what the Lord says about fear and anxiety in Philippians 4:6–7 (NIV): "Do not be anxious about anything, but in every situation, by prayer and petition, with thanksgiving, present your requests to God. And the peace of God, which transcends all understanding, will guard your hearts and minds in Christ Jesus."

If this fear is something you're dealing with right now, I would like to pause here and pray over you, if you'd allow me to:

> *God, we love You, and we thank You for how creative You've made us as human beings. You're creative, and You've made us in Your image to be creative too. I pray against the lies of the enemy that try to manipulate and distort that creativity for evil by allowing us to imagine all the things that could go wrong, creating fear in our hearts. I speak peace over our minds and hearts in the days and weeks to come. Show Yourself to us in a new and fresh way as we release any control we think we have over our situation.*

I pray for a peace that surpasses understanding to calm every heart reading this. I ask that You keep our babies safe in whatever way manifests itself. Help us to remember the gospel when we look at our children, to remember that as much as we love them, You love them even more. We know You have a purpose for the pain we face, and we thank You that we never have to wonder if You're good because we know You are. In the times we struggle to make sense of our situation, remind us of the times in our lives when You've been faithful to us. Help us to be a source of light to those who are hurting. In Jesus's name, I pray, amen.

CHAPTER TWELVE

RAINBOW SKIES AND FULL-CIRCLE MOMENTS

"Whenever the rainbow appears in the clouds, I will
see it and remember the everlasting covenant between
God and all living creatures of every kind on the earth."
—Genesis 9:16

A S MY HUSBAND AND I WALKED THROUGH THE PARKING LOT,
the glass doors of the hospital opened softly in front of us. It
was a familiar scene with an uncertain ending. Derek and I went
in for our very first ultrasound for this new pregnancy in March
2021. To say we were nervous would be the understatement of
the century. We were petrified. I had never experienced a healthy,
exciting, positive ultrasound. Like pregnancy tests, I only knew
ultrasounds to end in devastation. So, to try and imagine this
day having a happy ending sent me quickly into fight-or-flight
mode. I was struggling to trust the Lord. I kept teetering back
and forth between trying to have faith that God knew what He
was doing and thinking through worst-case scenarios. I couldn't
fathom what heartbreak would ensue if I found out I was losing
another child.

Before we left the house to go to the OB-GYN, we held
hands in the kitchen and said a prayer. I started choking up, so

Derek took over. He prayed for a healthy baby and a miracle and for everything to go smoothly. He asked the Lord to give us calm hearts and minds. He prayed peace over us. We left and drove to the OB office.

Our OB clinic had two locations, and I had vowed to myself never to go back to the same location where I had twice now received terrible news. So, we were at the new location. As we were sitting in the waiting room, my mind raced. There were moms walking into the waiting room holding car seat carriers. There were ladies waddling in with baby bumps that were "ready to pop" waiting to be seen too.

I'll never forget silently praying, *God, that's what I want. I want the baby and the car seat carrier. I want that outcome. I want to leave here knowing that in the next six months, I'll have that waddle. That in the next year, I'll have the little feet wiggling in the car seat.*

"Morgan Martin?" a nurse called. The sweet ultrasound tech made small talk on the way to our room. I gave complete but short answers back to her, and she could tell I was anxious. When I sat down on the blue chair covered in crinkly white paper, she said, "First pregnancy?" I responded "no" and told her briefly about our last ultrasound and how we had lost our first baby. She was incredibly kind and said she was so sorry for our loss.

Then, she was quick to squirt the wand with a little gel. She began to rub it onto my belly. When she turned on the monitor, we heard a *whoosh, whoosh, swish*. I felt butterflies everywhere. In my belly. In my fingertips. I was panicking.

The tech was very calm and talked us through everything she saw. She could tell that, at this point, ultrasounds were slightly traumatizing for us. Then, suddenly, there it was—a big black circle with a thin, long gray blob wiggling around on the bottom right-hand side. We could see the heartbeat as soon as she pointed it out. Derek started recording a video with my phone, and we just looked at each other, simultaneously taking what felt like the first real breath we had taken all day: a sigh of relief.

The ultrasound technician reassured us that everything was measuring correctly and that the baby looked great and healthy so far. We were so relieved. We stared at the ultrasound pictures nonstop on our walk back to the car. We laughed and reminisced about what the nurse had said and the funny little moves the baby had done on the camera. Derek drove us straight to Chick-fil-A for lunch to celebrate. (I mean, how else would you celebrate good news except by eating the Lord's chicken?) I snapped pictures of the little blob while we were in the truck. We hadn't told a soul about our pregnancy yet this time around, so I was bursting at the seams to tell anyone and everyone . . . I even told the poor high school kid working the Chick-fil-A drive-through that I was pregnant. With a half-confused smile, he said, "Congrats."

It was so surreal. After all the struggle, the pain, and the not knowing, I finally had closure. I could finally start seeing bits and pieces of why this had to happen, glimmers of redemption. I could see why this pain was necessary. I never would have had *this* baby if it wasn't for my loss. There's no way *this* baby would exist if it wasn't for the pain I went through. I knew God must have a huge plan for this child. Having this baby, that was my happy ending. Just months before, I'd had absolutely no idea how the Lord was going to work any of this. But it was turning out to be better than I could've imagined.

NO SUCH THING AS COINCIDENCE

My OB called the next day and told me my due date had changed a bit since the baby had measured just slightly ahead. She gave us our baby's new due date: November 16, 2021.

You may remember that it was in the early hours of November 16, 2020, that I was in the hospital, losing our first baby. The handprints of God were all over this. It was another glimmer of redemption in my story. My rainbow baby.

If you're not familiar with the phrase, "rainbow baby" is a nickname for a healthy baby that's born after the loss of a child. The phrase comes from the idea of a rainbow showing up at the end of a storm, a symbol of hope after trials and loss (Chertoff 2018). Our rainbow baby was due on the same day we lost our first baby, and I knew it wasn't a coincidence. This was the Lord showing up for me again to prove He would honor His promise in redeeming my story, that my pain wouldn't be for nothing.

In April of 2021, we found out our rainbow baby was a little boy. Our hearts were so full, and we couldn't wait to meet him. After my miscarriage, I often questioned if my body was somehow broken. I spent my entire second pregnancy in awe of what my body was able to do to grow a human. It was just so cool to me. Every ache and pain I felt during pregnancy was a reminder that God was keeping His promise to me. During those nine months, I was in such a place of gratitude. I learned what it truly meant to be grateful for things I wouldn't normally notice or that I would usually complain about. But this time, I saw all of the inconveniences and annoyances of pregnancy through a different lens, the lens of blessing.

I was thankful when my clothes stopped fitting. I was thankful when I started to see stretch marks in places I didn't even know could get stretch marks. I was thankful for weight gain, the kicks that kept me up in the middle of the night, the heartburn. (Okay, I wasn't thankful for the heartburn, I'll be honest.) I was thankful that I got out of breath when I made my bed or tied my shoes. And I was even thankful for the pain. The pain was as mental as it was physical.

The last year of my life had been one of growing and stretching in every way imaginable, and I saw how God had never left my side during any of it. I had constant access to Him, even when He didn't feel near, and especially when it didn't seem like He cared. Because I know that He did. This was proof, if I ever needed it before, that God is a God of His Word. He keeps His promises to us to never leave, forsake, or abandon us (Deut. 31:6 NIV). And he continued to redeem parts of my story.

We had maternity pictures taken at the end of September. It was the same week I had found out I was pregnant the year before. I wore two bracelets in my maternity shoot that honored our first baby. One of them was a thin gold bracelet with a pearl in the center that my mother-in-law got me as a gift in June 2021, which would've been the month I gave birth to our first baby. The other was a thicker silver band with black outlines of eucalyptus leaves covering the outside. On the inside, it read, "I will hold you in my heart until I can hold you in my hands." It was important for me to have a tribute to our first baby and our entire journey that led us to that moment represented in those maternity pictures.

Standing in a light-blue, floor-length dress on the hardwood floor of our friend's farmhouse studio, I tucked my hand under my very round belly. The sun was shining brightly on my face.

My baby boy was doing somersaults in my belly. Our first baby was ever present in my heart and symbolized around my wrist. I thanked the Lord.

With every click of the camera, I became more and more aware of how the Lord had allowed me to stand in that place. I thanked the Lord silently as I turned my head and looked into the camera again with a smile. Our story felt redeemed. It was all a reminder that God can redeem us from the most broken, hard, dark places we find ourselves in . . . if we allow Him to show up in our midst.

Maybe you don't see your glimmers of redemption yet. As the storm rages on, maybe the rainbow still seems impossible. All I can tell you is this: don't give up on God. He's working, even when you can't see it. Even if I had never gotten pregnant again, I would've still been called to trust God's plan. I would've still believed in His promises. I'll never stop being thankful for my rainbow baby, but that isn't the only path to redemption. God's redemption in your story is going to be uniquely yours. My prayer is that you have the courage to trust Him to guide you through your storm and toward whatever He has waiting for you beyond it.

CHAPTER THIRTEEN

HEALED HEARTS AND

FULL HANDS

"Therefore we do not lose heart. Though outwardly we
are wasting away, yet inwardly we are being renewed day
by day. For our light and momentary troubles are achiev-
ing for us an eternal glory that far outweighs them all."
—2 Corinthians 4:16–17

I T WAS 2 AM ON MY DUE DATE—NOVEMBER 16, 2021. I WOKE UP
with what I thought was just a really bad stomachache. I stum-
bled into the bathroom, turned on the dim light over our shower,
and saw evidence of impending labor. While my husband was
still asleep in our bed next to Nala, I jumped in the shower. I
practiced the breathing exercises I had learned, but the pain intensified. When I got out of the shower and dried myself off, I
changed into the set of clothes I wanted to wear to the hospital.
Once I was dressed, I decided to lay back in bed to try and get
some sleep, something else I had been told to do by our doulas.
The surges intensified again and were now time-able. I woke Derek up and asked him to call our doulas. It was around 3 am when
we notified them that I was in active labor. I wanted to labor at
home as much as possible, so we waited until about 5 am to head
to the hospital.

I was immediately put into a room where they checked my and our baby's vitals. Both of us were doing great, and they confirmed that we were, indeed, having our baby that day. Our doula met us at the hospital about 30 minutes later. After I was given my epidural, we talked with the sweet nurses who were in and out of the room all morning checking on us. They saw on my charts that I was exactly 40 weeks pregnant.

They were somewhat shocked that I was actually going to have a due-date baby. That's when I told them about what had happened exactly one year ago that day. I told them about how it was the same day we lost our first baby due to a miscarriage. I told them all about how the Lord gave us hope when we saw that our rainbow baby was due on the same date that we had lost our baby the year prior. Now we knew that our rainbow baby wasn't just due on that date; he was actually going to come on that date too.

We checked into the hospital around 6 am, and by 11 am, I had started pushing. But after four and a half hours of pushing (yes, four and a half hours) with very little progress, we made the decision to do a C-section for the health of the baby and myself.

At 5:48 pm on November 16, 2021, our rainbow baby boy—Brooks Cannon Martin—was born, exactly one year after we had lost his brother or sister. He had Derek's dark hair and piercing blue eyes, just like we had always hoped. He had the biggest cheeks (he got that from me) and little arm rolls. He weighed eight pounds, 10 ounces and was 20.5 inches long. He couldn't have been more perfect.

Looking back on that day, I had so much fun. People think I'm weird when I say that, but I just remember being so full of joy. I remember laughing and cracking jokes with the nurses. I remember our doulas being there, although only one was scheduled to be there. We had already told them both about our loss and the due date. So, it was special that each of them got to be there that day, witnessing the miracle of our story unfolding. The day my son was born was truly one of the best days of my life.

Even though I never wanted a C-section or an epidural, and the birth didn't go at all how I had planned, looking back, I can't think of anything I would've changed about that day. I have such fond memories of our birth story and how everything happened, and I think it's just another testimony to God's redemption, turning that day from tragic to beautiful.

God is a God of the details (Ps. 37:23 NIV). He didn't just redeem my story flippantly; He did it with intention. He displayed His glory that day in the hospital. We got to share our story about how this used to mark the worst day of our lives with the nurses and my OB and how it now marked the most redemptive day of our lives. There's no accident or coincidence that it happened the way it did.

Not only did God align everything so perfectly for my due date to be November 16, but He also allowed me to give *birth* to our miracle baby on that day. Not only that, but my husband also got to be with me, both of our doulas got to be there, my OB, whom I love and respect so much, performed my C-section, and my baby boy was healthy. God didn't just make that day okay. He made that day the best it could've been in every possible way. The wait was finally over, and November 16 will always hold a special place in my heart now for two reasons—my loss and my gain. Now I can't look at Brooks without remembering the goodness of God.

WHAT ABOUT ME?

Maybe right now, you're thinking, *That's really great for you, Morgan. But what about me? I don't have my rainbow yet or might never. What about my story?* I may not know much about you. I might not know where you grew up or who your parents are. I don't know your best friend or who you turn to for help. I may not know your struggles or all the other things in life that have caused you pain up until this point. But the God I serve knows even the number of hairs on your head (Luke 12:7 NIV). He cares so deeply and intimately about you that every tear you've ever shed is held in the palm of our Almighty God (Ps. 56:8 NIV). You aren't forgotten, even when it feels like it.

Your circumstances aren't a measure of God's love for you. When we go through pain, it doesn't mean God loves us any less or forgot about us. Psalm 139:1–4 (NIV) says, "You have searched me, Lord, and you know me. You know when I sit and when I rise; you perceive my thoughts from afar. You discern my going out and my lying down; you are familiar with all my ways. Before a word is on my tongue you, Lord, know it completely." You're seen, known, and loved by God even when it feels like you've prayed the same prayer for years and God doesn't seem to be listening, even when you thought you'd feel more healed than this by now, but you don't yet. Even when the pain still hurts, He's there. And His love hasn't deserted you or wavered.

Sometimes, bad things just happen. And sometimes those terrible things just happen to really good people who didn't do anything wrong. It isn't a consequence of something we've done. It isn't a thing God made happen to us. It just happened, and we don't know why. And sometimes, things just *don't* happen. Sometimes we pray for a baby or a miracle, and it just *doesn't* happen.

Life just isn't fair. It's full of uncertainty and unanswered questions. There will always be things that happen to us that don't make sense. In John 16:33 (NIV), Jesus says, "In this world you will have trouble." Unfortunately, that means we don't have to go looking for it. We can just keep living, and trouble will come and find us. You've felt this way, right? Like trouble has shown up on your doorstep, uninvited, and let itself in?

There are so many questions that I'm still asking, and I'm sure you are too. Questions that I don't have the answers to—for me or for you. I don't know why your story is going the way it is or why mine is, either. I don't know why you only had to wait a week to get pregnant again, and I had to wait four months or why you might still be patiently waiting for your rainbow baby two years later. I don't have all of those answers.

You may be wishing your story looked like mine. Maybe to you, my story looks easier or simpler than the hand you've been dealt. But I wish my story looked like someone else's too. I wish my story were easier. Even though I see the good in it now, I wish that I didn't have to go through a miscarriage at all. I don't know why our stories happen the way they do or why miscarriages had to be a part of them. But I do know that I wouldn't have Brooks if it wasn't for my miscarriage, and I can't imagine my life with any other baby than him. I never would've been able to experience the birth and life of this baby without the loss of our first. The timing of my story and of yours is divine and perfect.

UNIQUELY YOURS

Your story is uniquely yours. My story is uniquely mine. We are all on our own journeys, walking our own paths through this life. We can relate to one another on a surface level because we have had a miscarriage, yes. But that doesn't mean we can all relate to every single part of each other's stories. Our lives and backgrounds and experiences are all different, and they've shaped each of us into who we are as women today. Your journey is your own, and it will have its own unique ending.

Using your story, you'll be able to reach people that I never could with my story because of the life you've lived. You have a certain value to offer that I can't because of what we've each been through. But your unique story will only be helpful if you speak about it. Miscarriage is becoming a lot less taboo to talk about these days, thankfully. When I went through mine, so many people I knew closely sympathized and told me they had lost a baby too. Before that, I had no idea what they had gone through. Miscarriage happens so often to so many women every single day. My hope is that you use your unique story and whatever the personal, redemptive version of your story looks like to create cultural shifts. I pray that we use our pain of losing a child to bring back the value of human life in our society.

If you haven't seen your prayers answered yet or seen the redemptive work of God outwardly displayed yet, as I have, it doesn't mean that the redemptive work isn't happening. There's beauty in the incompleteness of our stories. There's hope in the in-between.

CHAPTER FOURTEEN

UNWAVERING LOVE AND

UNFINISHED BUSINESS

"And I pray that you . . . may have power, together
with all the Lord's holy people, to grasp how wide
and long and high and deep is the love of Christ."
—Ephesians 3:17–18

I WOULD BE REMISS TO SPEND THIS ENTIRE BOOK SHARING MY faith with you—and how the Lord redeemed our story—without telling you how I got here. When I was young, I grew up in church. We were there all the time, and it was so much a part of my childhood. When I was little, a Sunday school teacher told my class about heaven and hell. She said that those who know Jesus by praying a certain prayer will go to heaven, and those who don't will go to hell when they die. *Yeesh.* So, I repeated some words that someone told me to say because I just wanted to go to heaven. After all, the alternative seemed much, much worse. There was no real change of heart or desire for the Lord that followed.

For the next ten or so years, I lived life on my own terms, doing my own thing. I still went to church, and all my friends from school did too. I wasn't the kid who did drugs or got drunk or snuck out. I was, overall, a "good kid." That was my goal, and I thought that was enough. I wanted to be good enough for my own standards, make my parents proud, and earn God's love. Until one day when I realized that's not how it works, and I actually gave my life to Jesus.

I can look back now and see how the Lord was working on my heart then. I started really thinking about heaven and hell. As a junior in high school, I realized I would be graduating soon and then going off to college, and then who knew what else I'd do after that? But that impending milestone had me questioning what I wanted to do with my life and where I would be when it was over. I started really considering my relationship with the Lord and its authenticity.

Up until that point, my relationship with God had been very transactional. *If I do this for Him, He'll do this for me.* It was a give-and-take mentality. I expected everything from Him but wasn't willing to change my actions to serve Him. I wanted what He could give me more than I wanted more of Him.

The Bible says the fruits of the Spirit (attributes or virtues that are represented in your life as evidence you're a follower of Christ) are love, joy, peace, patience, kindness, goodness, faithfulness, gentleness, and self-control (Gal. 5:22–23 NIV). The Bible also says, "Each tree is recognized by its own fruit" (Luke 6:44 NIV), which means that our life should bear those fruits of the Spirit if we're truly connected to God. My life didn't. I knew what the Bible said, and I knew that my life didn't reflect Jesus behind closed doors as much as I pretended it did in the show I put on at youth group for others to see. Behind closed doors, I was living life for myself. The truth was that my spiritual life was dry at best. I had become really good at faking the whole "good Christian girl" thing.

On the night of May 3, 2011, I was in my room in my childhood home in northern Mississippi when I started praying in fear that my whole childhood had just been a show instead of a true change of heart. I was a "good girl" and did all the "right things," but did that come from a heart that knew God and desired to be like Him? Or did that come from a heart that wanted to earn God's love and approval by doing things to appear a certain way for others without a true inward transformation? I knew the answer . . .

That night, I prayed for the first time in a long time. I asked God to speak to me through His Word. I picked up my Bible, closed my eyes, opened it, and put my finger down randomly on the page. I opened my eyes. My finger had "randomly" landed on Ephesians 2:8–9 (NIV), "For it is by grace you have been saved, through faith—and this is not from yourselves, it is the gift of God—not by works, so that no one can boast." In the five seconds it took to read that verse, everything I had based my salvation on up until that point was demolished. I was trying to earn God's approval through good works. But the Bible says that our good works aren't the *basis* of our salvation. In other words, we can't earn salvation through being good enough. Our good works are the *evidence* of our salvation (Col. 1:10 NIV). Said another way, it means we don't do good things *so* we can be saved; we do good things *because* we're saved. We do good things because we understand the gravity of grace and God's goodness. That activates our desire to do good works.

Growing up in church, I also knew the verse that said, "And I [Jesus] give unto them eternal life; and they shall never perish, neither shall any man pluck them out of my hand. My Father, which gave them me, is greater than all; and no man is able to pluck them out of my Father's hand" (John 10:28–29 King James Version). I knew that if I had truly given my heart to the Lord all those years ago when I was a kid, I couldn't lose that salvation. I knew that even if I walked away from the Lord in the years in between, He would always be chasing me down to bring me back to Him (Matt. 18:12 NIV), and I would still be His child (Luke 5:11–32 NIV). But if I had never truly given my life to the Lord, then I was never in His hand to begin with. And that's what I began to wrestle with.

Maybe you're reading this and are blown away at how different our stories are. Maybe you're thinking, *Of course, God can forgive you, Morgan. What you've done isn't all that bad. You have no idea what I've done or what I've been through.* You're right. I don't know. I'm not sure what your life has looked like leading up to this moment as you're flipping the pages of this book.

Maybe you're reading this whole book with shame because you think that your miscarriage is a punishment or consequence for your choices. Maybe you're reading this, and you don't actually believe in God at all. You don't buy the Jesus thing, and you don't think He's real. Guess what? That doesn't matter. None of it. Did you know Jesus *still* loves you? He does. And I don't mean in the cheesy, cliché bumper sticker kind of way. I won't say Jesus loves you and take it back when I realize what you've done or who you are. No. You're loved, seen, valued, and worthy *just* the way you are. Jesus loves you, and He doesn't care what you've done or where you've been. Neither do I.

Maybe this whole God thing is new to you, or maybe you grew up in church like I did. Maybe you're familiar with stories in the Bible, and you've heard of faith, but it's never taken root in your life or caused a transformation for you. Maybe you're like me, and you've been trying to earn your salvation, and that verse above from Ephesians cut you as deeply as it did me.

Or maybe you were burned by the church or someone in it. Maybe something or someone at some point along the way caused you pain, and you walked away from the Church because you knew you didn't want to be a part of something where "those" types of people were produced.

I don't know what your life was like up to this point or what pains you've endured that maybe no one knows about. I don't know what grief you carry around with you day after day or what burdens you're lifting that make you feel like you may crumble beneath the weight of them at any given movement. I don't know what horrible things you've done, and I don't know what good deeds you've done.

But I do know that we have some things in common. It's likely we've both experienced a loss of some kind—which is why I wrote this book and why you're reading it. We've both done really bad things. We've both done really good things. Something else we have in common is that none of the good things we've done are good enough to earn God's love, and none of the bad things we've done are bad enough for Him to withhold His love from us. The love of God that's available to us both is a raw, unfiltered, untethered, no-strings-attached, constant kind of love.

THE ULTIMATE REDEMPTION

Greater than His desire to redeem your story of miscarriage, loss, and pain is God's desire to redeem your life. Better than God redeeming my miscarriage is His invitation to redeem humanity, and He offers this invitation to you too.

I'd like to share with you the true version of the gospel of Jesus and the hope that can be found in Him. This isn't a watered-down, incomprehensible grace that God freely offers for us to accept (or reject) at our choosing. This isn't me asking you where you want to go when you die. This is me offering you a life of abundance in Christ while you're still alive on earth. My goal is to share with you how you can live a life of peace, trust, and faith in the midst of the tragedies you've faced and any grief in your life that's to come.

John 3:16 (NIV) says, "For God so loved the world that he gave his one and only Son, that whoever believes in him shall not perish but have eternal life." I understand the gravity of this verse even more now that I'm a mother. I can't imagine giving my son up for anyone or anything, much less for a fallen people who turned their back on me. But God did. He sent His Son, Jesus, to earth for us so that we could be made right with God and have a fuller life here on earth and in His presence in heaven.

Why do we need to be made right with God? The Bible says, "For all have sinned and fall short of the glory of God" (Rom. 3:23 NIV). This proves that we have something else in common—the need for redemption.

We're broken sinners, but Jesus is perfection. Philippians 2:6–8 (NIV) says, "[Jesus] Who, being in very nature God, did not consider equality with God something to be used to his own advantage; rather, he made himself nothing by taking the very nature of a servant, being made in human likeness. And being found in appearance as a man, he humbled himself by becoming obedient to death—even death on a cross!" Jesus did that for you, for me.

You're so loved by the God of the universe that He was willing to give up His Son so that He could live in harmony with you. Maybe you can't fathom that love because the earthly representations of that love have been distorted for you by your spouse or your earthly father. But God is a constant God who doesn't change, as we've seen in previous chapters. You're loved by Him in spite of the things you've done or will do. Romans 5:8 (NIV) says, "While we were still sinners, Christ died for us." He didn't wait for us to become perfect to love us or give his life up for us. He also doesn't ask that you get your life and your act together before coming to Him for forgiveness.

When Jesus went to the cross, the Bible says, "For the joy set before him he endured the cross, scorning its shame, and sat down at the right hand of the throne of God" (Heb. 12:2 NIV). *You* were the joy that was set before Him. When He was going through the bruising and the beating and the pain and the suffering, and as He took His last breath, He thought of you. And He thought of me. He desires a relationship with us. It's love that we can't earn (Eph. 2:8–9 NIV). So, if we can't earn it, how do we accept this free gift of salvation?

"If you declare with your mouth, 'Jesus is Lord,' and believe in your heart that God raised him from the dead, you will be saved. For it is with your heart that you believe and are justified, and it is with your mouth that you profess your faith and are saved" (Rom. 10:9–10 NIV). Just like any other relationship, communication is key. It's a simple acknowledgment of our shortcomings and our desperate need for Him.

Understanding these truths for myself, I truly gave my life to Jesus for the first time. I finally understood the invitation the Lord was offering me and His love for me, though I still couldn't grasp His love fully. I gave my life over to Him on that night by simply asking Him to be the Lord of my life. I prayed and asked Him to be in charge of my life and gave Him permission to work in and through me and my life however He saw fit. There were no special words I prayed and no special words that you need to pray. I just talked to Him like He was my friend. I confessed my sins and shortcomings to Him (that He already knew about) and agreed with Him about my desperate need for Him.

As much as I desire that God redeem your story and restore what you lost in your miscarriage (and I have faith He will), I more so desire that He redeem your *entire life* if He hasn't already. This is an invitation available to everyone. His love is given freely and without discrimination. If you're someone who has walked away from the Church because of an unfortunate circumstance and vowed to never do that "Jesus thing" again but read this book in hopes of finding some form of healing for your situation, I encourage you that true and ultimate healing can't be found outside of Jesus. I also urge you not to let imperfect Jesus followers (or people who claim to be followers) tarnish the perfection that is Jesus Christ Himself.

It's no mistake that you're reading this book here and now at this very moment and that you've made it this far. God wants a relationship with you. He doesn't want the rituals you've inherited from your parents because your whole family is "religious." He doesn't want the acts of service, like being in church every week without the true heart transformation. He desires a personal relationship with you, and all you have to do is accept that invitation and allow Him to be ruler over your life. Choose to submit to Him and seek His authority on the decisions you make.

If that's something you've never done before and you desire to do that now, there's no pressure. Just talk to Him. If this is your first time ever praying, just imagine you're chatting with a friend across the table over a cup of coffee. Talk to Him like that, and remember He knows your heart and doesn't need fancy words or language to hear your prayers. He just desires your heart. 1 John 1:9

(NIV) says, "If we confess our sins, he is faithful and just and will forgive us our sins and purify us from all unrighteousness."

I extend to you the invitation I accepted over 11 years ago that has truly transformed my life in every way. I'm not a perfect person because of that decision, and I never will be on this side of eternity. But the Lord is doing work in my heart and making me more like Him every day. Now, when I go through hard times, I'm able to rely on the Lord to be my strength. I ask Him to heal my heart and give me faith that He is still good, even in the midst of the storms of my life that don't *feel* good at all.

When people asked me how I was able to be "so strong" during my miscarriage, I know it wasn't because of me. It was Christ that became my strength when I didn't have any left. "That is why, for Christ's sake, I delight in weaknesses, in insults, in hardships, in persecutions, in difficulties. For when I am weak, then I am strong" (2 Cor. 12:10 NIV).

I don't know how people face trials in this life without a foundation of God to build on, to fall back on. You don't have to. Jesus walks through our pain and suffering with us. That doesn't mean He just makes the pain, or fire, go away. It means He sustains us through the fire. Living your life for Jesus doesn't come with the promise of an easy life here on earth. It's a way to have hope in the midst of the pain we'll inevitably still face. "I have told you these things, so that in me you may have peace. In this world you will have trouble. But take heart! I have overcome the world" (John 16:33 NIV).

If God has the power to redeem our lives, He surely has the power to redeem our stories. He can make our shattered lives and souls whole again. He can use our tests as a testimony. He can turn our pain into purpose—if we surrender to Him and allow Him to do so.

God sent Jesus down to earth to die on the cross, rise again three days later for us, and offer us the free gift of eternal life. We also see in scripture that God is coming back, and there will be a new heaven and a new earth (Rev. 21:1 NIV), "So you also must be ready, because the Son of Man will come at an hour when you do not expect him" (Matt. 24:44 NIV).

Right now, we're living in the in-between. Isn't that a place you know well? We're living in a time after His death and resurrection but before He comes back again. Yet, we still see the Lord moving and working. We still see Him showing up in unexpected moments, His grace and His love poured out over us in the unfinishedness of the gospel. We see the start of His story and His redemption, but we won't see it in full until He comes back for us.

In the same way, we can see that there's beauty and redemption in the unfinishedness of our own story of miscarriage. And just because you may not have that baby yet, or the healing you've been praying for, we can rest assured that God is still moving. He's still working, and He's still showing up. The gospel won't just be beautiful when it's finished. It's beautiful even now. So is your story. There's beauty in the moment we find ourselves in now. There's joy in our waiting both for the Lord and for our blessing.

CHAPTER FIFTEEN

BABY BOTTLES AND LASTING LESSONS

"See, I am doing a new thing! Now it springs up; do you not perceive it? I am making a way in the wilderness and streams in the wasteland." —Isaiah 43:19

P AIN DOESN'T COME WITH A ROADMAP. I WISH IT DID. I WISH we had something to guide us along the way to tell us how to feel in each moment and how to carry ourselves. If there was a roadmap, there'd be a little key at the bottom that would tell us how to get through the first holidays without our baby or how to endure their first would-be milestones. But the truth is, there's no right or wrong way to feel. There's no right or wrong road to take. At times, you'll feel absolutely numb, and other times you'll feel a whole flood of emotions all at once. At times, you'll know just what path to take, and other times you'll struggle to get out of bed. And it's all okay.

If you're at the beginning of this journey, I want you to believe that you're going to smile and laugh again. Your pain won't always be so messy or raw. I still remember several months after my miscarriage, when I tucked myself into bed one night and realized I hadn't thought of my miscarriage *at all* that day. That was the first day in a long time I was just a "normal" person going about my day. That's how I knew my heart was in its process of healing. I couldn't forget about what had happened, but I was moving away from the stage where it alone defined who I was. I was getting used to my new normal.

If you're in the middle, that desert season, the gray area, I hope you see this book and the lessons from the Lord as a turning point in your journey toward healing. I hope you're reminded that this isn't the end—the desert season is only bringing you closer to your promise. This is an essential piece of your journey that will lead you to your ultimate destination. You're in this season now, but don't stay there. It serves a purpose, but this isn't the endgame for you. God has so much more He wants to walk you into. Lean into who you're becoming and who God's creating you to be. You'll need it for wherever He's bringing you. I pray you don't settle for the wilderness when God can give you the Promised Land. I've shared countless stories in this book from my own life and from the Bible of how the Lord has come through and been faithful.

I don't know what God has in store for you specifically or how your story will end. But what I *do* know is that God didn't include all those stories and miracles in the Bible to show you what you can't have. He's calling us to bigger and greater things. He has a huge purpose for our lives and can create beauty from ashes.

He's showing us through all of these testimonies what not settling looks like. We've seen testimony after testimony of people like Hannah, Shadrach, Meshach, Abednego, the disciples, the crowd of five thousand, Elijah, the Israelites, and so many others who trusted that God would bring about miracles. They earnestly sought for the Lord to give them more of Himself. They weren't okay with average or good enough. They wanted more. May we be like them and refuse to settle. I pray that we trust the Lord to bring us from this gray season to a season of abundance, overflow, and more than enough.

If you're moving out of the desert season into a season of motherhood now, I hope you don't forget that the God who brought you through the trials of the desert is still the same God who will continue to provide for you in this new season. The same God who was teaching me and showing me the way during my season of mourning and grief is still the same God who shows up for me now that I'm a mother. He's still teaching me new things in light of my new role. He uses my son to show me new things about Himself or things I've forgotten.

When my son wakes up in the middle of the night because he's hungry, he starts with small grunting sounds, just enough to wake me up but not enough to turn into a cry yet. When I hear that grunt, I go ahead and start fixing his bottle so I can feed him because I know that's what he needs.

Of course, it isn't a surprise that he's hungry. I knew he'd need a bottle before the night even started. But I couldn't give it to him when he wasn't hungry yet. Instead, I waited until I knew he was ready to receive it. But I had washed the bottle earlier that day in preparation, knowing it would be needed later.

While I make the bottle, I talk to him in a soft voice and remind him that I'm there and going to help him. But because of his position in the room while I make the bottle, he can't see me. So, he has to rely on my voice and have faith that, because I'm near to him, the food is coming. That grunt quickly turns into a scream and a cry of panic and discomfort because it's not coming fast enough. But it takes me extra time because I have to make sure the water is warm enough to soothe him but not too hot to scald him. I also have to make sure the measurement of the formula is proportionate to the water in the bottle and an appropriate amount for his age. When I finally finish making his bottle, I carefully pick him up and whisper to him as I feed him, "Mama's here, baby. You don't have to cry. I've never not fed you when you were hungry, sweetheart."

And God simply whispered back to my heart, *Yep* . . .

HE KNOWS YOUR NEEDS

When we ask the Lord for things, it's not because we have to enlighten Him to our needs. He knows our needs, but He desires *communication* with us. When we ask for those things according to His will and His glory, we don't usually receive them in that exact moment. But He's working behind the scenes preparing things before you even know to ask for them. He's making sure they're given to you exactly as they should be, in the appropriate proportion, so that it doesn't harm you but actually benefits you!

He will always be there for us. We simply have to trust that His nearness to us means He knows what we need. The silence in that exact moment doesn't mean He can't hear our cry or that He stopped caring for us. God loves you too much to answer your prayers at any other time than the right time and in any other way than the right way.

"Which of you, if your son asks for bread, will give him a stone? Or if he asks for a fish, will give him a snake? If you, then, though you are evil, know how to give good gifts to your children, how much more will your Father in heaven give good gifts to those who ask him!" Matthew 7:9–11 (NIV) promises us.

And Philippians 4:19 (NIV) reminds us, "And my God will meet all your needs according to the riches of his glory in Christ Jesus." God already knows what you need, and He's working behind the scenes for you so He can provide for you at just the right time.

God doesn't change, even when our circumstances do. As we look back on all the history of the Bible, we see that He remains constant. He was faithful to Adam and Eve; faithful to Hannah; faithful to the Israelites; to Shadrach, Meshach, and Abednego; and faithful to me for all my life. As I look back on the stones I've set up to remember His faithfulness, I see that the stones aren't few.

He is a gracious God who never leaves us or forsakes us (Josh. 1:5 NIV). He has never wavered. He is the same God that was there for me during my parents' divorce. The God that was there for me during my miscarriage is the same God that's been there for me during my first year of motherhood.

I want you to know that God doesn't abandon us when things get hard or overwhelming. He doesn't show up for the good times and leave when it's bad. He sees your vulnerability not as an opportunity to manipulate you for His benefit but as a platform to display His glory and grace in your life. He's a constant, faithful Father whose biggest desire is to grow closer to you and help you become more like Him.

We can worship God despite our heartache. It's hard to do, especially when worshipping feels like the last thing we want to do, but worshipping in the midst of misery truly ignites the healing process.

In the midst of my worship throughout this process, God healed my heart. He took away my grief and filled me with a new sense of hope for my future. He met me where I was because I chose to worship Him despite my heartache. I learned through His acts of grace in those moments that I could trust Him with my grief and worship Him in the gray area, knowing He's still good. We can rest in knowing He has a plan for our lives "to prosper you and not to harm you, plans to give you a hope and a future" (Jer. 29:11 NIV).

SO, WHAT NOW?

Now's the time to pray big, bold, audacious prayers. I was challenged to do this myself throughout my own journey. When I started asking God for specific things, He began showing up for me in specific ways. We know that praying big prayers doesn't mean that God will answer them how we want Him to. Prayer is a gift to us that God offers so that we can communicate with Him, a relationship He so freely offers. In praying big prayers, we remind ourselves that nothing is too big for God. We acknowledge our need for Him and ask Him to help us in our situation. When we pray big, bold prayers, we agree that God is big enough to accomplish what we're asking Him for and trust that He's still good even if He doesn't.

Surrender your situation, your timing, and your plans to the Lord. I know that it's hard to surrender, and it's much easier to surrender our timing than it is to surrender our plans. I pray that you see God is worthy of your full surrender. That you'll show up daily and choose to release both your timing and your plans into His capable hands. Knowing what we do about His love for us and His unwavering character, I encourage you to put your faith in Him. I don't know how your story will turn out, but I know the One who does. And I know it'll end in a way that displays His glory and will be for your highest good.

Maybe you're like me, and you're on the other side of this middle area now. You're on the other side of the desert regarding miscarriage. Maybe your miscarriage happened so long ago that you have grown children now. Maybe your situation isn't like that, but you've somehow come to the place where you've crossed into your Promised Land, into your healing, and maybe you need this truth of surrender to apply to other situations.

Now that I'm in my Promised Land, I still have to surrender to God in other areas. I have to surrender my baby and his safety over to the Lord. When I first had my son, my attempts to keep my son safe were a bit more vigorous than most moms. For the first month or so after he was born, I struggled with postpartum anxiety, something about 15 percent of mothers who have experienced miscarriages may experience, according to the American Psychological Association (Leis-Newman 2012, 56). I was so afraid of losing my baby that I lived in paralyzing fear of all the things that could possibly happen to him. It was a very isolating and helpless place to be. But control is ultimately elusive, and that's why surrender is so important. Surrender means relinquishing that false sense of control and giving the reins back over to whom they truly belong. Surrender is a constant acknowledgment that God's ways are better and higher.

MY PRAYER FOR YOU

My biggest hope and prayer for you is that you find God worthy of your trust, just as I have. In doing so, you can surrender both your plans and your timing to Him but also surrender your life to Him.

I pray that you'll see that what He offers in a life with Him is truly more freeing than in a life apart from Him.

I pray over every set of hands that touch this book, including yours. I pray that the Lord will redeem your story and give you beauty for ashes (Isa. 61:3 NIV). I pray that He'll turn your mourning into dancing (Ps. 30:11 NIV), and I hope that you see the redemptive hand of God not only in my story but also working in your own life as well.

When your heart is broken, when tragedy strikes, who's the first person you turn to? When that all-consuming anguish fills your soul, who's the one you confide in? My prayer is that you begin, if you haven't yet, to run into the loving arms of Jesus, who loves you so much and uses even the worst moments of your life to build your character and bring you into the promises that have your name on them.

I hope that you find peace through Christ and the words He chose to fill this book. And my greatest desire is that you'll place your trust in God, not the vices of this world, for your healing. I pray that you'll cling to Jesus during this time of heartache and in every season—joyful or painful—that's to come. In the act of surrender, allowing God to redeem every piece of who you are and will become, you'll see that He's already begun healing your empty hands.

ACKNOWLEDGMENTS

THIS BOOK IS THE PRODUCT OF A DREAM THE LORD LAID ON MY heart in January of 2021. A special thank you to everyone who made my dream and obedience to the Lord come to life.

Jesus, thank you for the hard seasons. Thank you for the way you show up in them every . . . single . . . time. Thank you for giving me a vision for something so big that I never would've had for myself. You never grow weary of helping me look more like you and less like me. You've promised in your Word never to leave me or forsake me, so thank you for being a promise-keeper. I see your hand in every single minute of my life. You've been there. Thank you in advance for how this book transforms lives, perspectives, and hearts for the kingdom, in *your* name and for *your* glory.

Derek Martin, my husband, my rock, my biggest supporter, when I told you about this wild idea to write and publish a book, you never wavered in your encouragement. You picked up the slack where it was needed to provide me with the time I needed to invest in this book being written and published. This book was just as much a commitment for you as it was for me. I love you more than words could say. I'm thankful to have you as a life partner and best friend. I wouldn't want to walk through "for better or for worse" with anyone else but you.

Mom and Dad, you've walked with me since the literal beginning of my life but especially through this journey. You were by my side every step of the way. You both cried with me, checked in on me, and helped me heal. Thank you for always encouraging me to dream big and telling me time after time that I can do anything I put my mind to. Because I believed you, I wrote a book.

My friends, you never told me my dreams were too big. You always pushed me to start and to finish this journey. You've been patient in my times of silence while I poured my heart and soul into this endeavor. You have shouldered my pain in the valleys and celebrated with me on the mountaintops. God created us for community. I'm thankful you're mine.

My book coach, Ashley, you taught me how to write a book and helped me believe in myself throughout this entire process. You helped me overcome impostor syndrome and accomplish the feat of writing this book in just 18 days. I'm forever indebted to you for how you've changed my perspective and my life. Thank you for helping me live out my purpose and my calling, one page at a time.

To my editors and publishing team, thank you for seeing this book for what it was and what it could be. Thank you for your grace in not throwing my original version in the trash can. You took the bare bones of my creation and helped me breathe life into it, allowing this book to make a stronger impact on the life of every reader.

To you, my friend, the one holding or listening to this book. I feel connected to you without even knowing you. Thank you for trusting me enough to pick up a copy of this book. Know that my heart and soul are on the pages of this book, and I hope that anything I've said has helped you find comfort in the midst of chaos. You're not broken. Your story isn't over, and I want to thank you for taking the time to read mine.

ABOUT THE AUTHOR

MORGAN MARTIN IS A SOCIAL MEDIA INFLUENCER, WIFE, MOM, and dog mom. She wrote *Healing Empty Hands* after her own experience with miscarriage to help women find redemption, discover purpose, and praise a good God through life's greatest heartbreaks. Morgan is passionate about toxic-free living and being the healthiest, best version of herself! After her miscarriage in November 2020, Morgan became passionate about helping other women who have struggled through the same painful experience and providing resources that weren't yet available to her during her healing. She currently lives near Grand Rapids, Michigan, with her husband and her beautiful rainbow baby, Brooks.

To learn more about Morgan, please visit *www.healingempty-hands.com* or find her on Instagram at @morganreneemcintyre and Facebook at facebook.com/morganmcintyreadventure.

To contact Morgan regarding speaking engagements, media inquiries, or with any other questions, please email healingempty-hands@gmail.com.

BIBLIOGRAPHY

Attenborough, Richard, director. *Shadowlands.*
　　Price Entertainment, 1993. 132 minutes. *https://www.*
　　roku.com/whats-on/movies/shadowlands

Chertoff, Jane. 2018. "What is a Rainbow Baby?" Healthline.
　　December 6, 2018. *https://www.healthline.com/health/*
　　pregnancy/rainbow-baby.

C.S. Lewis. AZQuotes.com, Wind and Fly LTD, 2022.
　　Accessed August 10, 2022. *https://www.azquotes.com/*
　　quote/1351684.

Kierkegaard, Soren. 1938. *Purity of Heart is to Will One Thing.*
　　New York: Harper.

Koenig, Harold G. 2001. *The Healing Power of Faith: How Belief*
　　and Prayer Can Help You Triumph Over Disease. New
　　York: Touchstone.

Leis-Newman, Elizabeth. 2012. "Miscarriage and Loss." *Monitor*
　　on Psychology 43, no. 6 (June): 56. *https://www.apa.org/*
　　monitor/2012/06/miscarriage

March of Dimes. 2017. "Miscarriage." Last modified November
　　2017. *https://www.marchofdimes.org/complications/*
　　miscarriage.aspx.

Platt, David. 2013. *Follow Me: A Call to Die. A Call to Live.* Illinois: Tyndale House Publishers.

Portelli, Maria Teresa. 2016. "The Benefits of Prayer on the Physical and Psychological Well-Being." Universe of Faith. May 31, 2016. *https://www.heritage.org/civil-society/report/prayer-good-your-health-critique-the-scientific-research.*

Robert Wood Johnson Foundation. 2020. "Miscarriage of Stillbirth Increases Risk of Breakup or Divorce." November 17, 2020. *https://www.rwjf.org/en/library/articles-and-news/2010/11/miscarriage-or-stillbirth-increases-risk-of-breakup-or-divorce.html*

Sloan, Richard, Harold Koenig, Start Butler, Cynthia Cohen, and Christina Puchalski. 2003. "Is Prayer Good for Your Health? A Critique of the Scientific Research." The Heritage Foundation. December 22, 2003. *https://www.heritage.org/civil-society/report/prayer-good-your-health-critique-the-scientific-research.*

Spurgeon, Charles. "Weak Hands and Feeble Knees." The New Park Street Pulpit Volume 5. Royal Surrey Gardens: March 20, 1859.

Made in the USA
Monee, IL
05 March 2023

29233431R00095